So That

For Relationships

Jennifer Andersen Smith

Get the *So That* Journal Free!

Go to www.jenniferandersensmith.com
to download your free copy of the Journal now.

The events and conversations in this book have been set down to the best of the author's ability, although some names and details have been changed to protect the privacy of individuals.

Published in the United States of America by
Jennifer Andersen Smith
www.jenniferandersensmith.com

Table of Contents

Dedication

This book is dedicated to all of you who heard part of my story and said "you should write a book".

I could not have completed this project without

The strength and wisdom of my God,
The absolute and infinite support of my husband,
The inspiration and encouragement of my kids,
The love and hope of numerous family members and friends.

Love,

Jen

The "So That" Principle

Introduction

The "so that" principle is a twofold purpose for why you are here on this earth. It is 1) to learn and heal for yourself *so that* 2) you can pass on to others what you have learned. As we move through life, we all desire to find purpose. Having a purpose in life helps us to feel as though we matter and can make a difference. Without meaning, the suffering and pain in this life is so much deeper than we can ever imagine. However, God, in His infinite wisdom, has provided us with purpose in order for our human minds to make sense of the suffering and pain we experience.

The principle is found in verse 2 Corinthians 1:3-4 of the New Testament of the Bible.

Blessed be the God and Father of our
Lord Jesus Christ, the Father of

1

mercies and God of all comfort, who
*comforts us in all our affliction **so that***
we will be able to comfort those who
are in any affliction with the comfort
with which we ourselves are
comforted by God. 2 Corinthians 1: 3-4

This verse simply says that God shows us mercy and comfort in our pain **so that** we can pay that same comfort and mercy forward. We are commanded in this verse to share our comfort with others. As a part of sharing that comfort, we must also share our experiences and afflictions. We, as humans, are told to love one another and to comfort one another as God Himself has done.

This life is temporary and, as such, we need to process the experiences we have pretty quickly. If we don't process our painful experiences adequately, we tend to develop bitterness or anger. On the flip side, if we don't process our joyful experiences properly, we stand to lose out on much of the joy those experiences could bring to us. These will also provide joy to carry us over the troubled times we will inevitably endure.

How to know if you have processed your experiences enough is quite simple really. Do you feel joy from positive experiences even though much time has passed? Has your pain eased, and has peace come forward, in your feelings about negative experiences? Feelings of remorse signal that we need to forgive ourselves, while feelings of bitterness show we need to forgive another person. Are you able to provide comfort to another person in similar circumstances as you found yourself?

There's a saying "those who can, do and those who can't, teach". That saying has always bothered me. If you can do something, why wouldn't you not only do it, but then also teach it, pass it on? This is what parents do every single day, even if they don't mean to. Children first learn by simply mimicking those around them.

Next time you're with a baby, move your face in different expressions, the child will attempt (to the best of their ability) to make the same movements. Make noises to the child, the child will make noises back to you. This is foundational learning and sharing. This is the heart of God's commands to love and comfort one another in the way He loves and comforts us.

Remember, forgiveness does not mean we have let someone "get away" with their transgressions. Whether we are the transgressor or the transgressed upon, forgiveness means we can move forward in a productive way in our lives to face the next experience, and that we can do so without traces of the transgression continuing to color our feelings and decisions. Should we always show such compassion, caring, kindness just to risk being hurt again? Yes, but also no.

Forgiving someone does not mean you become a doormat and let this person run you over again and again. Forgiving someone means you no longer hold that transgression against them, but you can also arm yourself against the same behavior.

You, as a human, do not have the power to fundamentally change another human. You can only change your reaction. If you choose to see the good in someone, that's great, but if you choose to ignore the way they hurt you so that you can only see the good, that's not healthy for you long term.

I learned this principle through a wise and learned Sunday school teacher from many years ago. She was in my life for a season of time and showed me how to learn what I needed. How to stay grounded in my God's word and in my own self. She came into my life a few years before I finally acquiesced that my marriage was over. And, in so doing, what she showed me in the Bible and of our human experience was an intricate part of my processing the pain and sorrow I would feel as my marriage ended, as my daughters each went through crises, as old friends fell away and new ones entered. As life changed so dramatically for me, I kept the phrase "so that" forward in my mind. I knew that God had a greater purpose in everything I experienced.

It's not so much that God gives or allows certain painful experiences to happen. God is an all-loving, all-knowing God who loves me and all His children deeply.

As a sign of that love, He gave us free will. This free will allows us to each choose how closely we will align our lives with him through prayer, Bible reading, and meditation. I'll be the first to admit, I have not always aligned myself closely.

At times, I have strayed so very far as to be unsure how to get back. The beauty of God is that even if you stray to the ends of the earth, He is always right there, inside you and beside you, ready to take your hand at your sincere, honest request. God is a benevolent God who suffers and is hurt at the painful experiences involved in our human experience. Especially those events that occur due to our actions against one another.

As the concept of this book came alive, and as I wrote it, I hoped it would help others understand the "so that" principle. I'm getting a bit ahead of myself so let's go back to the beginning and see how I got here.

Chapter 1

In the Beginning

I had an idyllic childhood. I was raised on a small farm that was an easy bike ride outside of the small town of Sycamore, IL. The fourth child and second daughter in birth order, my childhood was during the 70's and 80's. My parents were both raised on farms where their parents actually farmed the land, so it was natural for them to desire a larger homestead instead of an in-town lot. Both my parents worked full time jobs outside the home, but also kept up a large garden and orchard as well as caring for various animals through the years.

We had many different dogs and cats. Willie, Stephanie, Max, Trixie and Daisy were the dogs. Mostly the cats were not named but my little sister had one particular gray kitten that she called "Mouse". Willie is the first pet I even vaguely remember. He was a chocolate lab that moved from Virgil to Sycamore with us, but he ran away during the first winter after the move. That would have been the winter of 1975-76. Even though I don't really remember Willie, I do remember asking my mom about where he went. I asked my mom if we could track him in the snow the next year when it snowed again.

I guess my little 5-year-old brain thought the tracks would show up again in the next snowfall. I was hoping. Needless to say, Willie was never seen or heard from again. Many years later I asked my dad about him and his best guess was that he must have been hit by a vehicle on a road somewhere.

When it came to playing with the cats, mostly my sisters and I would annoy them by making them do tricks and keeping them in different boxes or cages while we played with them. But they were barn cats and not really pets; they had a job to do just like every animal on a farm. Their job was to keep the mice and other barnyard pests to a minimum in the barn and around the house.

Other animals we had through the years varied from horses to ducks to sheep to pigs to cows to chickens. Some of the animals were named—Laverne, Shirley, Lenny and Squiggy, to name a few. We had a set of pigs once that were called Mike and Ike. Every proper farm needs a rooster so we had one too. His name was Chicken George and he was mean, vicious and angry. He actually came from my Uncle Joe, but I'm not sure if he was a gift or a curse.

One sunny afternoon when I came home from school, I went into the barn to let the dog off his chain. I think that was Max and he was prone to running away during the day so we chained him in the barn in a way that he could get outside some and reach his food and water. But, as long as someone was home, he would stay home so we'd let him off the chain in the afternoon.

My brothers were home and I went to the barn to unhook him. But Chicken George was out in the main area of the barn and decided to mess with me. As I tried desperately to unhook Max, Chicken George kept fluttering into the way and scaring Max. Then Max would shy away and I would lose my grip. Max decided to fight back and chase the chicken. As he chased, he wound the chain around my legs. Mind you, my legs were bare because my Catholic school uniform was a dress, so the chain starts to scrape and cut my skin. I yelled and yelled for my brothers to come help me.

Somehow, I finally got Max unhooked and then unwound the chain from my legs. All the while I continued to holler for help. I finally made my way into the house and asked my brothers why they didn't come to help me, to rescue me. They said they never heard me, then they said they did hear me but they thought I was singing. Singing, what? My singing sounds like hollering? At that moment I don't know what upset me more: the pain in my legs or my brothers believing that my singing and hollering sounded the same.

We were expected to go to church on Sundays and dress appropriately. No jeans or tennis shoes mainly. No t-shirts either. When we got older, we were allowed to go to later Mass, but we had to bring back a bulletin to prove we had gone. Such a silly thing really because we could have grabbed a bulletin on the way in and circled around and gone right back out. But that was the deal.

We were expected to help around the house for the girls; around the barn and yard for the boys. I was always jealous of that. Of course, who knows, I may have hated it. But, as it was, I wanted to be outside working with the plants and flowers. In the sunshine. However, every Saturday, we cleaned the house. Rosie would usually offer to clean the bathroom.

We had one bathroom for all of us. The bathroom was pretty big though. Probably measured 10x10 or more. I remember we each had our own drawer in the cabinet. Mine was on the bottom of the row because I was the youngest girl. I can still see my hair ties, ribbons and paraphernalia in there. And Mom used Mary Kay for years. I can see her pink pots of potions she kept in her drawer. I would open them and look them over. Just to see.

As siblings we were expected to pitch in whenever something needed to be done. We didn't fight much from my perspective. But I know my brothers are like oil and water. Just two very different people. I remember my dad and one of my brothers fighting a lot. This was largely because they were two very different people. Looking back at it now, I can see they most likely were both super frustrated with each other.

I loved it when I got to do whatever I wanted. My sister Rosie and I did lots of performing on our driveway stage. The driveway was elevated from the yard by about 2 or 3 feet, so it made the perfect platform. I would use the jump rope with one of the wooden handles as a microphone and put on concerts. Jump ropes and their handles make perfect microphones with wires. Often performing to my imaginary crowd. Mom and Dad didn't come sit for the performance. I don't remember ever finding Mom spying on me or anything. I felt free and alive as a child.

And then, my world got dark and claustrophobic.

As a prepubescent, I was sexually abused by a boy 6 years older than me. It happened more than once. He told me that he had learned about sex in health class and wanted to experiment. I was his guinea pig. I was about 8 years old when this started. I know this because the west room in the upstairs was still painted green and a toy room. Thus, it was not yet my older sister's room, which means my younger sister wasn't old enough yet to move upstairs. It is strange the details one remembers from these episodes.

He touched me in places no 8- or 9-year-old wants to be touched. He looked at me, as though inspecting me. I remember vividly one time in the hayloft. He would hold me down and breathe his milky smelling breath in my face. He would fondle my chest, which was completely flat, so I didn't get what he was doing. I wondered why he would do that. I remember feeling yucky after each encounter, but he always told me that was okay.

He began to taunt me with the actions. We would see each other on the bus and occasionally when he would find me out and about on my own. He wanted me to tell the other girls on the bus what he was doing to me. He threatened to do these same things to my sister and to the neighbor girls. I had to protect them from this same ickiness that he brought whenever he was around. I definitely didn't want anyone else feeling this same way.

I knew what he was doing was wrong, but we didn't talk about things like this in my family. We were a good Catholic family who went to church each Sunday and followed the priest's teaching. How would I ever even come to my mom with this? Besides, when it wasn't happening, I put it out of my mind as quickly as possible. In all likelihood, I put my mind elsewhere even when it was happening.

For years, I held this all inside and wondered what made me an easy target. Was it because I was the youngest girl in the neighborhood? Was it my naivete? I trusted him; he was a friend of our family. Why wouldn't I trust him? Remember too, this was in the 70s; we were not as aware with our children as we are now.

He would be in our house or yard because he was friends with my brothers. He was completely trusted. No one had a reason to suspect anything. He groomed me well. I probably had a crush on him at some point, although it makes me nauseous to think that now. But he was an older boy who would pay attention to me—who wouldn't like that? As a younger sister, and the youngest child for many years, I may have been a bit slighted on attention, or at least thought as much.

I know one time we were in the barn together. A usual occurrence. This time we were looking for the new kittens Dad had said had been born. My sister and I loved playing with the kittens when they were old enough for us to do so. We had to be very careful to not disturb them too much until Dad gave us the ok. He and I climbed the ladder to the loft and then I crouched down looking in all the crevices for the nest of kittens. I don't know how it started, but it did and what I remember is lying on my back with his face over mine. His breath always smelled of stale milk. Not sour or bad milk, just stale, old milk.

I remember fearing pregnancy. He told me I couldn't get pregnant. He told me something about menstruation, but I didn't really get it then. I had not started. I do remember thinking in my bed late at night, this means I won't be a virgin on my wedding day. Raised as a devoted Catholic girl, this was upsetting to me. I wanted to be that girl that saved herself for her husband. But he stole that from me. I do think he stole much more from me for a time, yet I've moved forward and left a lot of that in the past. He stole choices from me. The choice to be a virgin on my wedding night, the choice to enjoy sex as part of a loving, fulfilling marriage. This is what God intended with sex, not the perverse mockery our world makes of it.

Several years ago, on the advice of my then therapist, I set up a meeting with my family to tell them about this. I asked my brother to host the meeting at his house rather than at my mom and dad's - where I grew up, where the abuse took place. It was a weekend afternoon in the fall. We all came together - Mom, Dad, brothers, sisters, spouses. No children of course. I told my story. Read it from the pages I had written, which I still have.

When done, I remember pleading with my brothers not to do anything to this person. I knew he still lived in the immediate area, thought it likely they would see him from time to time. I had learned he was married with two young daughters. My brothers said I should report this and my response was that I was not going to do that. I had dealt with it, this meeting being part of my process and therapy. They implored me to do so, to think of the others he might be doing this to, or future victims. While I would hate to think he continued that behavior, I had to put myself first at this time. I had to be ok with my decisions. My decision was and still is not to report publicly who this was or what happened.

I found out at this meeting that he did this to my sister. After finding out he had done it to her, I wondered if he did it to the other neighbor girls because he threatened to do this to them too.

Those who read this book from my hometown may be able to deduce who it is. Let those chips fall where they may. He has to live with what he has done to my sister and me. He has never sought forgiveness from me, and I have no desire to face him.

I don't feel animosity or hatred, I just feel nothing. Like, this was a thing you did to me, I wish you hadn't because it forever altered my life, but you did. You have to live with that shame and sin, not me. Maybe he is a Christian who has been washed of his sins. Maybe he has helped others who have done these heinous deeds. Maybe not. But I cannot carry that with me. That is on him and him alone. Forgiveness is not for me to grant or withhold. That's between him and the one true God.

I learned that bitterness and anger can control you even when you don't know it. My sister has said she is not bitter, but her words have betrayed her. That day, during this meeting, she was very angry and bitter. Even though on that specific day she said she wasn't bitter. I tried to help her, but she was not in a place to listen as the pain was too much for her that day. I was not strong enough to help her. We have only spoken of it a couple of times since that day. Each time, I hear anger, resentment, heat, towards this person.

While I understand the reason and believe she is justified in her feelings, I wish she could find a way to resolve it for herself. I believe that some of this bitter and resentment is the root of at least some of her health problems. Correlation between anger and illness has been made through research. I'm not certain that causation has been linked, but correlation certainly has.

Years ago, I watched a documentary about women who were abused in a Catholic girls' school as children and teens. One woman told her husband about it and she believes wholeheartedly that the reason he developed throat cancer, and subsequently died from it, is because he kept swallowing the rage and bitterness that he held towards the men who did it and the women who allowed it. She tearfully explains in the interview that she had begged him not to do anything or say anything as it would embarrass her. Her words left no doubt that she relates her request and his acquiescence directly to his throat cancer.

My first husband couldn't handle this once what exactly had happened came out. He had thought it was much less physicality than it really was. Of course, when I first told him about it, I was 16 or 17 years old, that good Catholic girl who didn't talk about sex or things of that nature. I most likely left a lot of holes for him to fill in as he imagined.

When I did finally tell him all of it, we had been living in Atlanta for a couple of years at least so that would put us at 32 or so. I had hoped he would have been equipped to handle it better. I do think that may have been the beginning of the end of our marriage. We had more counseling since that time than ever before. And we had gone to 5 counselors over the course of our 23-year marriage.

This put up a big wall between us emotionally that neither of us could figure out how to get past. There were a couple of times after this that I felt suffocated during our intimacy. I know that freaked him out. Can't really blame him for that. But all I needed was compassion and understanding and most importantly space. He did quite the opposite. In the last 10 years of our marriage, it was a constant battle for more sex. The harder he pushed, the farther away I pulled. I didn't want to give up that control and he didn't understand what his actions were doing. Of course, hindsight being 20/20 is super helpful.

When I was a teen, Moonlighting was a popular show starring Cybil Shepherd and Bruce Willis. I loved that show. But Dad wasn't a big fan because they had sex on that show. And they were not married. He mentioned it once at the dinner table which was very strange but looking back, I think that was his best attempt at the sex talk with his teen daughter that he was clearly concerned about. He just wasn't equipped with how to have that conversation.

As I sat there listening to Dad voice his concerns, my thoughts were that it didn't matter anyway. I had already had pre-marital sex as an 8-year-old with the neighbor boy. It was too late for me. I was a bad kid, bad Catholic, bad person. I wish I could honestly say I never lied to you, but I know I did that day when I told you I wouldn't do that anyway because I knew it was wrong.

Hindsight being 20/20, that would have been the perfect time for me to say oh yeah, by the way, I'm not a virgin and the kid down the street, not my current boyfriend, is the reason why. But really, how could a naive girl say that to parents who didn't talk about these things? I don't remember having a conversation with my mom about my changing body even, let alone the next phase of physicality in my life after puberty—sex.

Just the same as my sister showed me where the makeup was and her version of how to use it, my sister showed me where the feminine products were kept and what to use.

This lack of conversation led me to be very open with my little sister about my pregnancy and the actions that led to it. We were driving into town shortly after my pregnancy had become known. Just she and I in the car.

She asked me something about the baby and I used that opening. My older sister and I had both talked about making sure our little sister had that talk even though we had not. I think that later helped us to have the hard conversations with our own kids.

Man, I can remember sitting in my daughter's room as she was a junior or senior in high school and talking about the ramifications of sex, physically and emotionally. But I was more so focused on physically and making sure to avoid disease and pregnancy.

Being Forgiving

This abuse affected me in multiple ways throughout my life. How would I say the "so that" principle was applied here? I learned how to forgive someone of a grievous transgression yet not let myself become a doormat through that process. Examples of that can be seen in the later years of my marriage and as I matured in my career.

Since I knew I couldn't be a virgin on my wedding night, I willfully participated in sex as a teen. While I don't know for certain I would not have done so if I had not been sexually molested, I also can't say for absolute I would have. I believe this led me into teenage pregnancy, because I had nothing to lose really. My virginity was stolen. As a child or teen, I did not understand the deeper essence of God's mercies and becoming new again through His divine grace. So I kept on and became pregnant at the age of 16, had my first child at 17.

Don't get it twisted, I love my children 100% and they know this. But I would not recommend teenage motherhood to anyone. I truly believe that because I have been close to my God throughout my life, He has continuously guided me as a parent. As such, I have four of the greatest kids a parent could ask for.

One of my goals as a mom was to have all my children graduate from high school without becoming parents first. I crushed that! Ha! All my kids graduated and were out of school for at least 5 years before blessing me with grandbabies. (Let me tell you, there really is nothing like being a grandma!) Have I made mistakes with them along the way? Absolutely. 100%. No doubt in my mind. But, through the Grace of God, they are all fantastic, productive, self-sustaining adults.

I believe that my curiosity about sexual acts is borne mostly from this abuse. I believe I've spent times in my life trying to find out what the bigger part of sex is all about rather than seeing it through the eyes of the abuse. Surely it must be more than just this physical act. I do know there is power and vulnerability in the action. I have never been a big fan of sex. I don't doubt at all that is due to the initial experiences I had with the act. He didn't know anything radical or kinky, but I knew what he was doing wasn't morally right, even as a child.

I learned how to understand that everyone is at their own healing process and pace. My own sister has dealt very bitterly with this experience. While I cannot blame her for feeling that way, I can certainly wish better for her. I pray that she now feels peace by understanding the "so that" principle herself and learning to move forward. I can also take the time to truly understand, appreciate and validate my own feelings about this experience in order to be what she needs when it comes to discussing this situation, or not discussing it. That's love really. To be what others need us to be but still be honest and true. It's a fine line between becoming what they need us to be and staying honest in ourselves.

Many years ago, I received a phone call I had prayed I would never receive. A very close friend of mine has a daughter who was about 6 or 7 years old and she had fallen prey to a deviant person. This girl's older brother, probably only 12 or so himself, had decided to use her to experiment with his sexuality. Much in the same way I was used. This darling girl suffered from many side effects of the fear, misplaced shame and insecurity for years.

I remember immediately going to be with them as I felt I could maybe help in some way, just by understanding how their little girl might be feeling. As it turned out, I was just sitting silently with her dad and he asked me, "Jen, I just don't know what to do. What can I do?"

I held his hand, looked him in the eye and quietly said, "Keep her safe. She needs to know that Daddy will always be here to keep her safe, to hold her whenever she needs it, to comfort her whenever she is scared."

Daddies are very powerful emotionally for their daughters and I think most men don't realize that. They are busy in the day to day of providing for their families and the minutiae of just getting things done. But, dads, the most powerful, restorative, loving thing you can do for your girls is hold them and tell them in words and actions that they are safe and loved.

While in the midst of writing this book, I received another phone call that I absolutely hate to have received. More so, I hate that such a call had to be made by this sweet young woman. This kind, compassionate young woman called because she was recently assaulted by a young man she thought was her friend. She went to his house to hang out, which was a usual occurrence, and he proceeded to try to rape her. Thank God in Heaven that she was able to get out of there before it was completed. But, as is understandable, the situation completely traumatized her.

However, because of my experience, I feel that I was better equipped to handle the phone call than if I had not had this experience. I feel I was able to advise her better on her options and what her next steps should be than if I had not had my experience. Would I trade my experience and get rid of it from my life if I could? Absolutely yes in so many ways, but then I look at how I believe I helped these two young ladies and wonder, would I really trade it out and not be able to help them? I don't know that I would, I really just don't.

This is how the "so that" principle works. Because of my experience, and processing it through my faith in God, and the comfort He has provided, I am able to share God's comfort with these two strong young ladies. And for that, I thank God.

Chapter 2

Dating Teens

It was a lazy Saturday afternoon at the end of September, during my junior year of high school. My parents were gone for the day; in fact no one was home. I decided to take a nap, because, what else should a teenager do when left to their own devices? I took my current book and snuggled into Mom and Dad's bed with their satin comforter—so comfy.

About an hour later I was awakened by the phone ringing. Not a cell phone like we would have now, a rotary dial desk phone with very little control of the ringer volume. Since it was in the room with me, it startled me awake. Back then, you had to answer the phone to know who was on the other end. It was my best friend, Bobbi. She had just been on the phone with a mutual friend, Chris. He wanted to know if I wanted to date his friend Brent.

Well, my initial thought was something like, "Why didn't he call me himself?" So, I said no. He needed to call me if he wanted to go out with me. After discussing further to be sure that's the answer I wanted to give, Bobbi hung up to call Chris back. What you don't know is that I'd had my eye on this guy for a bit now. I had gone with him and Chris to a couple different football games and done some flirting in the classes we shared.

As my sleepy mind woke up, these thoughts became clearer to me and I called Bobbi back in a quick panic. I told her to call Chris back and tell him I changed my mind. She laughed and said she would call him back and tell him to have Brent call me himself.

When he called, he told me he hadn't called himself because he was nervous to call me at first for fear of rejection. I thought that was sweet. I told him I had been woken out of a sound sleep and that's why I said no initially. He laughed at that.

Our conversation was cut short though because he had to go to work. He was a delivery guy at Joey's Pizza, best pizza in our hometown. There was even a time or two I went with him for deliveries, until curfew. Since I was not allowed to date until I was 16, we had to do group dates for a few weeks. Chris rode along with us to make it a group. Such a good friend.

We had many adventures together. We went to many football games and then ate at Wolfenberger's after. At the beginning of our senior year we had some friends who had graduated and got their own places the year before. Then we had parties at their apartments. The first time I got drunk was at one such party. Bartles and Jaymes wine coolers are easy to drink. Sweet, smooth and delicious. You don't realize how much alcohol you've had until you go to stand up. At least, I didn't that night.

Oh wow, it was time to head home for curfew, but my head was spinning so bad and Brent was in no condition to drive. Thank goodness our friend Chris was around. He took me to a phone booth (no cells, remember?) so I could call home and make some excuse to stay out later. I was so anxious about being caught by the way I talked on the phone.

We had Agriculture class together. I think it was Ag 3, not sure. I also took the horticulture class, so my Ag projects were usually of the flowers and plants varieties. We both did dairy judging contests for a few years. We went on ski trips, with the FFA (Future Farmers of America) group and just with friends. Snowmobiling was another winter favorite activity.

We would go bowling at Four Seasons and play pool too. Often a friend would host a bonfire so we'd hang out there all night. We were both in FFA club at school. Our junior year we were both officers. Then, in our senior year we were voted as President and Vice-President so that was cool. Well, until it became known that I was pregnant.

Brent and I were worried for quite a while that I might be pregnant, but we had convinced ourselves that ignoring the issue would make it go away. Yeah, not so much. In November of our senior year, Mom asked me straight out if I was possibly pregnant. She had noticed my clothes weren't fitting as well.

I immediately broke down in tears and admitted it. I had been holding that back for so long, it was truly a relief to talk to Mom about it. She was highly disappointed in me, but she also made me feel like it wasn't the end of the world. Now we had to start talking about care, options, future plans.

One night we had a meeting at my folk's house to discuss the situation with Brent's parents. I remember his dad being there but I don't remember his mom being there. I'm sure she was, but I just don't remember her. We discussed the options available with the pregnancy. The future plans that Brent and I may have had were now altered. Certain options were off the table completely while other options were now reviewed.

During this meeting, and in conversation with Brent and my own prayer time, I decided I had to give the baby up for adoption. What was a 17-year-old kid gonna do to raise a baby on her own? I could just see a life of want and need in front of us both. This also changed my dream of being an architect. I had already been applying to colleges but now, those seemed to be far-off unattainable dreams. Unless I gave up the baby. Surely we could find a wonderful family to love him or her and give the baby a beautiful life.

During a Girl Scout meeting (yes I was still in Girl Scouts and trying to get my Gold Award. We had a small troop, only 3 or 4 of us. Bobbi was in the troop with me, we had been friends and in scouting together since elementary school.), we discussed what I was going to do. I told them all we were going to give the baby up for adoption. My scout leader asked me if that was something I really thought I could do. I admitted, for the first time, it was not. How could I live not knowing anything about this child and where he or she might be, what they were doing, how they felt? I was very unsettled with this decision now that I had had it questioned. For me, family has always been a very important part of my life. I'm a very traditional person with traditional values and upbringing.

After bringing it up with Brent, he was relieved. He did not want me to give the baby up, but also felt like he didn't really have the final say. He suggested we talk with his mom. She had given up a child around the same age in her life. Maybe she would have some insight. After talking with her about her experience, I knew I couldn't do it. The trick was having this conversation with my folks now and getting their support.

I think they were relieved too. This was their first grandchild and I don't think they really wanted to have him or her adopted away from the family. They were so incredibly supportive. They agreed to help raise the child until we could be out on our own. We moved things around in my room so we could make room for a crib. Decided to redecorate it, new paint, curtains, etc. The night I went into labor, I had to pull the protective plastic sheeting off my bed before I could go to bed. But, by the time I got home a few days later, it was all ready to go.

Brent was even allowed to stay at my house, sleeping on the couch, for the first few weeks after the baby was born. It was pretty helpful to have another person there. I was so not prepared to be a mom. Looking back now, at the age of 47 with 9 adult children and step-children and 9 grandchildren of my own, I realize just how completely unprepared to be a mom I was. I am so grateful that God provided all that he did to help me and the babies get through their childhoods with beautiful outcomes. In the end, the decision to keep the baby was the right one for us.

Within just a few months of the birth of my first child, I found out I was pregnant with child number 2. So, I was going to be a mom again and I hadn't even turned 18 yet. This was definitely not in my plan, but my actions led directly to it.

Why in the world did I end up pregnant again? Well, there is the obvious answer, the one my dad and brothers like to joke about. But it goes deeper than the physicality of the actions. There was emotion and immaturity tied up in the choices, or rather a lack of making active choices. I had just had a baby at 17, 2 months before I graduated from high school. I was still a teenager. I was still capable of making decisions that affected my future in ways I didn't consider because I was still a teenager. I tried to be smart and I went on the pill.

After just 6 weeks, I was convinced by a person older and wiser (or so I thought) that I shouldn't be on birth control. Looking back, I think he was really trying to convince me to abstain from sex, but I didn't grasp that at the time and just stopped taking the pill. And poof, I was pregnant again.

What should I have learned from this? Well, on the surface, some would say, I was not very smart and needed to be taught a lesson more than once, therefore, 2 pregnancies. I didn't get the lesson the first time.

The lesson, if you look at it that way, is to abstain from sexual behavior as a teenager or quite frankly, if you cannot handle the consequences. Physically, that could be a baby or a disease. But emotionally, oh boy, emotionally, this can tear you up. And for me, the decision was definitely more wrapped in the emotion of it all. Looking back, I know that I was participating in sex more so for fear of losing my boyfriend if I did not participate. Additionally, we never talked about birth control. I would venture to say that most teens don't. That's why it's so very vital for the adults to take the lead on these conversations. Even if you don't want your teen to be sexually active, and he or she tells you they're not, you still need to have the conversations with them. Help them find the resources they need to be protected.

It's the hard conversations we have in life that ultimately make the biggest impact. Maybe if I'd had an adult to talk to about it, who'd made me talk about it, I would have figured out the emotional component before I was pregnant the second time. Or before we got married, or before we had 2 more children, moved 800 miles away from everyone, or before we separated and divorced. Maybe.

Becoming Aware

So many lessons I learned through the first 18 years of life were not actually a part of my rational decision making until much later in life. Getting married at the tender age of 19, being a mom of 2 at this time, and trying to figure out all that those things entail left me with little time to sort through my thoughts. At the time, it was everything I could do to get through each day, as any mom of little ones will tell you.

Self-care is vital. I did none. When I became a mom and wife, I threw everything I had into it. I had been taught how to cook, I knew how to care of the babies, I could clean, do laundry, manage money. All the things I thought I should do. I was motivated to be the best I could for my children. I will be the first to admit that the focus should have been on my husband AND on my children, but it was easier to focus on the kids and their needs, so that's what I did.

If you find yourself suddenly in a position you didn't expect, take some time to evaluate the situation and your reaction to it. Make yourself get up earlier, stop at a park on the way home, stay up later, to deal with the situation. This is how you empower yourself. You take the 30 minutes out of the day that you need and focus on yourself. Focus on the way you are reacting to your current life situation.

Maybe you'll find that you are exactly where you want to be with no desired changes. I truly wish that for each of you. But I do think more people will find that they're not completely at peace with it and will need to dig to find out what changes would be better. The next step is seeing if those changes are even feasible. Talk with the people involved and get their feedback. Then go through the process again. Evaluate your situation, develop a plan to change it, take action, and reevaluate your situation.

My first marriage lasted for nearly 25 years. There is a lot about myself that I learned as I grew from a 19-year-old teenage mom to a secure professional of 44. As we journey through this book together, there will be many glimpses into my marriage. Sometimes, it may seem out of order chronologically, but I've done that so that it makes more sense.

First Mother's Day

My first child, Tony, was born in March of my senior year. As the weeks went by, we found our footing with this baby thing. I had decided not to nurse because, well, I was a 17-year-old girl. But I was still at home for several weeks on maternity leave from my senior year in high school. I was missing out on the last few weeks of schooling, missing my friends, missing the challenge of school. It was difficult because I didn't feel like me anymore, even though my brother and his wife had made it quite clear to me that just because I was having a baby, that didn't change who I was as a person. The person at my core was still me no matter what. But when you're stuck at home with a newborn and a tutor, it begins to feel like everything has changed. I began to look forward to any social activity. Even a simple dinner out, just to get out of the house.

My very first Mother's Day was quickly approaching. I was happily anticipating the day even though no 17-year-old girl thinks it will be to celebrate her entry into motherhood, but to celebrate her own mother and grandmothers. Brent began to tease me about the great Mother's Day gifts I would get. He would talk to our baby and tell him not to tell, to keep the secret. I began to really get excited about the day. I love presents, I love being celebrated and this sounded like it would be a second birthday each year. What could possibly be wrong with that, right?

That morning I woke up with great excitement, ready to celebrate my mom and grandmas but also to be celebrated too. As per usual for a Sunday, we started our day by going to church with Mom and Dad. I'm not sure, actually quite doubtful, that Brent came along. I do believe that some of my siblings would have come along. After church, we went back to Mom and Dad's to have a family celebration. I still lived at home. Brent, the rest of my other siblings, Grandma and Grandpa all came over to celebrate a beautiful spring day.

We all had brunch together and gave Mom her gifts, cards and flowers. If I remember correctly, that was the year we all went together and gave Mom her ring which she still wears. We were all so excited to be able to do this for her. We had the ring custom designed and Mom loved it. Watching her excitement built mine up too!

I thought it a bit odd that Brent did not give me any presents or cards at that time, but I brushed it off thinking he wanted privacy or something. We left Mom and Dad's to go to his mom's and still nothing. We visited with his mom for a bit and then he brought me back home.

We shared a quiet evening with my folks and some of my siblings. Then he went home. I remember feeling just shocked. What was happening? I hadn't even got so much as a "Happy Mother's Day" greeting from him, let alone a card, flowers or the simplest of gifts. Being so shocked I didn't process it at all, but I do vividly remember being awed that he could be so indifferent and quite frankly a bit of a liar.

I wanted to give him the benefit of the doubt, so I talked with him about it. I reminded him of the teasing he had done through our son and directly with me that heightened my excitement. He really had nothing to say. He didn't think he had done anything terrible and didn't think he should apologize for anything. He just didn't get it.

Looking back now, I think I was probably dealing with depression even then.

Getting Married

The day of my wedding was crazy hectic. Not at all what I thought it would be like. Every girl thinks about her wedding day to a certain extent. I really thought it would be more relaxing and calm.

My children were blessed to have a second mom, whom they call JuJu to this day. On our wedding day, JuJu cared for Tony and Norah. She met us out at Mom and Dad's in the morning and I didn't have another worry about them all day. After dropping off the kids, I picked up my dress and we all headed to the church and school. We used the kindergarten classroom of the elementary school as the place to get ready. It so happened to have been my kindergarten classroom 15 years earlier.

My Aunt Roxie met us at the school to do my hair. She made it all curls cascading down one side. I loved that hair style. I still love that I chose that style. Aunt Rox made it look so good too. Rosie, Teddy, Grandma Herrmann and Aunt Roxie all gathered with us.

I put my dress on. I don't remember this being a moment or having pics done during this time. At some point I went into the bathroom in the teacher's lounge do my makeup. I was alone. I remember it being very quiet.

The light in the lounge was off so it was a little dark. The light was off near the front desk and entrance to the school. The only light was that of the November sun shining. It was a bit weak if I remember correctly, a winter sun.

I was nervous, scared. I would label the feeling as anxiety now. Almost an out-of-body feeling. I can see myself in the bathroom doing my makeup with my little stash of Maybelline eye shadow and mascara. I'm pretty sure I did not use foundation or blusher at that time in my life. Just some eye shadow, mascara and maybe lip color of some sort.

As I watch myself get ready, I can feel this sense of dread creeping in, not so much the anxiety now. Anxiety implies more energy than I felt. My thoughts were quiet. Calm, steady. I would like to think that if someone had come to me in that moment and asked me if I was 100% absolutely certain to go through with this wedding, I would have said no. I don't love him enough to marry him for life. I like the idea of marriage. The traditional family setting of marriage, but really, I don't love him that much.

Looking back, I'm not sure I ever felt true love for him as a lover should feel. At first, I mostly felt infatuation and was in love with the idea of being in love. Many teenage girls feel the same way, but they don't get themselves in quite the same situation, so it doesn't impact the trajectory of their lives. I also felt a sense of responsibility for these children we created together. I had agreed to raise them when I couldn't go through with adoption.

I have always held a very traditional set of values. Raising a child means Mom and Dad are there, together. So I got married.

After the wedding ceremony, and millions of pictures, we had planned to drive ourselves to the reception in our fancy new Pontiac 6000. As we left the church, a light snow was falling. When we left the church, alone except for our best man, we realized no one had the keys! My purse had been picked up by my bridesmaids or parents in an effort to be helpful. Brent did not have keys on him for some reason and neither did Chris.

I can't remember exactly how we got ahold of anyone, but I'm sure it had to be before they got to Genoa for the reception because it didn't seem to be that long. This, of course, was long before everyone had a cell phone in their pocket. Eventually, we got a key somehow and made our way to the Vets hall in Genoa for the reception.

We had a full dinner downstairs in the Vets club. I don't know what we ate. The kids sat at a table with JuJu, right in front of us. There were the requisite toasts, merriment and family time. Before we ate, we cut the cake and fed each other. I'm thinking it must have been rather uneventful since I don't remember it.

Eventually, we made our way upstairs for the dancing. My brothers supplied my new husband with plenty of drink even though we were underage. He was hammered pretty early on. Tried to dance with me in a fashion that I never liked, just kind of gyrating and thinking he was being sexy. Not really anything I ever enjoyed or thought was attractive. It felt embarrassing really. I've always thought that was the Catholic school girl in me. Looking back, I think he just doesn't know how to dance any other way. I always thought it too closely mimicked sex. And therefore was embarrassing in front of family.

We did the dollar dance as well as the tossing of the bouquet and garter. By the time we got ready to leave, Brent was completely drunk and I'd not had a drop of alcohol. Maybe if I'd had, it would have been more fun for me.

As it was, I was now experiencing a new anxiety because I knew nothing about our honeymoon plans. I wanted it that way because I handled all the wedding items myself. It was the only thing I really asked him to take care of other than his own tux and his groomsman.

We had a town car pick us up. Brent stumbled in the back and promptly fell asleep. Luckily the driver knew to take us to O'Hare. We flew the red-eye flight to Vegas. It was a good thing I had stuck with my usual traveling plans and brought a book. I read my book the whole flight while he slept stretched out across the aisle, oblivious to anyone needing to get up or down it. Back in 1990, flights could be nearly empty but would still fly. This flight had maybe a handful of people. No one was around us. The attendants were nice as could be.

We landed in Vegas and I had to wake up my new husband from his drunken sleep. He finally awoke enough to tell me we were heading to our sister-in-law's in San Diego at Camp Pendleton. Yippee! I was so excited to see her and my niece and nephew. I hadn't seen them for some time. Bree and I would write long letters to each other to help get through whatever perilous phase our children were currently in. It was a real treat when our husbands would talk to each other on the phone so we could then do the same. This was back when long distance was expensive. The idea of spending a week there was very exciting. I had also never been to California or the west coast.

My darling husband slept on the second flight as well. We finally got into California and to our hotel for the night around 2am, California time. I had been up for nearly 24 hours straight. But it was our wedding night and I wanted to make it special. I was given an absolutely gorgeous emerald green gown with black lace—very sexy. The sexiest thing I owned, ever. I went into the bathroom to get ready. And, you guessed it, when I came out, he's sound asleep with no hope of being awakened. Out came my book once again.

The next morning, we headed over to Bree's and enjoyed a day with them. Saw their townhouse, played with the kids, did a little sight-seeing. Bree recommended we go to a restaurant called the Hungry Hunter or something like that. Brent and I went and enjoyed it greatly. Delicious food, yummy bread. Unfortunately, Brent's brother was in Japan doing a year overseas, so we were not able to spend time with him.

The second day we took the trolley to Mexico. That was an adventure and a half! Some of Bree's friends came too. I think the trolley ride took about an hour. When we crossed the border, they warned us to ignore the beggars and the people who confronted you to buy their wares.

I was not prepared for the sight of so many people sitting on the curb begging. I was a country farm girl from the Mid-West who ignored any homeless or panhandlers in the city, let alone seeing them in a different country and looking so incredibly poor. Their lack of decent clothing and shoes was pitiful. There so many children. This was different than the beggars in Chicago. Those are grown adults, typically men. The worst thing about their appearance is typically their teeth or hair looking unkempt.

We moved quickly through the streets to the market we were heading for. We did a little shopping but mostly just strolled through the market. We visited a rooftop bar where they gave us tequila shots and delicious margaritas. I don't remember doing the shots but I certainly drank my share of margaritas. Brent did the shot if I remember correctly, or someone from our group did.

The shots were given by the servers who would tip back your chair while you drank the shot and then they shake the living life out of you and rock your chair back to get your balance off. This had an immediate effect as opposed to waiting for the tequila to set in. We saw many college kids who ended up on their butts because of these drinks.

I remember buying a short and tank top outfit. We also bought a blanket. Both items were very scratchy. Brought them home and washed them several times to soften them. We bought goodies for the kids, a set of maracas I still have. Gifts for Teddy and JuJu who were the primary care givers for our kids while we were gone.

Upon our arrival back at home, we settled back into our life together. As you will see in the passages to come, there are moments of beauty and joy as well as moments of confusion, sadness and hurt. As I look back on my life, I choose to remember the moments of beauty and joy as opposed to focusing on the harder parts. There are lessons in all the moments if we are looking for them.

Becoming Conscious

I didn't realize it at the time, but I was learning not to trust my husband through these experiences. It was so subtle I didn't realize for years that I did not trust him. In the early days, I thought I was in love and that love could overcome any concerns, any issues, any worries. I know that to be untrue now.

Love can certainly overcome a lot of issues. But, if you have that love without trust, is it really true love? I say no, it is not.

There have been times in my life that I have loved the Lord but not trusted in Him. Without trust, love means very little because you cannot grow together. The kindness and patience of love is diminished, the tolerance of love is destroyed when trust is not present.

As we move through the scenes of my life, we can see a pathway emerging. This pathway is not straight and narrow. It is wide and turning, twisting back on itself even. Sometimes we have to experience things multiple times in order to learn the lesson or get the good from it.

Chapter 3

South Cross Apartment

Our very first apartment. We moved in during August of 1989. It was on South Cross St in Sycamore. The rent was government subsidized, Section 8 I guess, at $444 per month for us. It was a lot for two kids fresh out of high school and only one full-time job, a baby and another on the way. But, along with the help of family, we managed it.

The apartment was on the ground floor with 2 bedrooms, 1 bath and a ginormous master closet. We considered using it as a nursery for the new baby since the second bedroom was pretty small. The laundry room was communal in the building's hallway. A sweet older lady lived across the hall. Our upstairs neighbors liked to vacuum at 2am and weird times like that. Luckily, Tony didn't wake up for that.

We were pretty happy there. We had three different couches during that time. One was an ugly rust-orange couch with rough fabric, the next one was a cute floral couch that I loved. My mother-in-law bought it for us from Goodwill for my birthday. The last one was a blue set we bought from an auction my uncle did. It was a couch and loveseat that lasted us for many, many years. Brand new! It's so exciting to get brand new furniture. And as an 18-year-old, I felt very adult making that purchase.

Brent had begun to develop a good relationship with his father through Tony's existence. Something about that third generation began to form a bond, a common interest finally between father and son. John was a good man with his own faults, just like each of us. He worked hard, kept to himself, but there was great love for his family always. Brent has that same great love for his family too. He inherited that from both of his parents and it was a big part of what kept us together as a couple for so long.

On a beautiful June evening, my future father-in-law showed up unexpectedly at our apartment. Brent was working because at the time he worked for DelMonte. It was harvest time. During harvest, Brent would work from middle of May to middle of October and would often get no more than 1 day off per month.

That evening, I had started working on a little dinner for myself and Tony while he played in the living room. John unexpectedly appeared over the railing of the patio to our apartment. He called hello to Tony through the open patio door. We quickly let him in the apartment and had a wonderful evening. He played with Tony and held Norah. We had a simple dinner and enjoyed each other's company. This was on a Sunday night and we had no idea that it would be the last time we would see him.

Just a day or two later, John had gone to work that morning like he had every morning for many years. He was the courier for the company which meant he drove the van from the company campus to the post office, airport and everywhere in between. Whatever needed to be picked up, whether person or parcel, and delivered elsewhere, was his responsibility. He truly enjoyed his job. He also had a plan to retire soon and buy an RV. He was so excited about that idea, as excited as an extreme introvert will show you anyway.

That morning when John got to work, he ran his usual errands and then was called into his boss's office. He went readily assuming it was just another task for his list. However, it was completely the opposite. He was being let go. The company stated it was because they were concerned with his driving record and if he had the ability to continue to drive safely for them. He had apparently been in a couple of small scrapes, no major damage and no injuries, in the previous quarter. John was so upset by this news that he refused a ride home, took his belongings and started walking.

That day was very warm and very humid for a June day. I had just taken the babies for a walk in the stroller and was drenched with sweat and humidity. While trying to unlock the door of the apartment I could hear the phone ringing. This was a wall phone, way before cell phones were so popular. I left the kids in the stroller in the hallway while I rushed in to grab the call. It was Brent telling me the terrible news.

Apparently, when John was walking home, he suffered a heart attack and fell in the ditch. He was not found until later that afternoon when the factory next to his former employer had shift change. One of the factory workers saw him lying there and tried to help, but it was already too late. That day changed so much for the trajectory of life.

If Brent had had more time with his father to solidify that relationship, I believe Brent would have been a different, emotionally stronger person. As it was, he now had twice been stunted in his attempts to develop a relationship with his dad. Once, when he was about 9 and his parents split up, and now, at the vulnerable time of being a new dad himself.

Stonehenge Apartment

A few months later, we moved into an apartment on Stonehenge for $550 monthly rent. We lived there for several years, not moving until August 1994. When we moved in, Tony was 17 months and Norah was 5 months old. Brent's dad had passed away 2 months earlier.

The apartment had much smaller closets and it was on the second floor. There were only 4 apartments in the building, which was set slightly into the ground like a split level. The lower apartments had to go down about 4-5 steps to get to their units while we had to go up about 8 steps to get to ours. The laundry was in the hall downstairs.

Both Tony and Norah were in diapers at this time as they were not potty trained until about their third and second birthdays respectively. I mostly used cloth diapers for them because of the lesser cost compared to disposable diapers. I was home with them anyway. I tried to do couponing when we lived there. Since I wasn't working, I figured it was my contribution to the family.

Now looking back, my contribution was being an at-home mom because that avoided the cost of day care, work clothes, a car for work, lunches, etc. At the time, I didn't like it though. I was 18 years old and this was not necessarily the plan I had for this time. Instead of moving into a new apartment, I should have been moving into a dorm room at SIU and entering my second year studying architecture.

But I wasn't there and I wasn't afforded many opportunities to use my brain in the way I had been using it every day at school. I swear to you I could feel my brain turning to mush daily. Just melting down inside my skull to nothing but the most basic instincts and language. Toddlers will do that to you. I've learned that it doesn't matter if the mom is 18 or 38, they have this amazing power. However, toddlers also have this power to love and show complete and unconditional adoration.

While living there, we got married, we had a third child, we bought our first cell phone—which I hated Brent for doing because it was so expensive. We bought a new car while living here: a Pontiac 6000. A sedan with a sports engine. It was the showroom demo and Brent was proud of that car. He used his inheritance from his dad to buy it. We had that car for many years. I loved it and didn't really want to get rid of it when we did, but we needed a bigger vehicle and couldn't afford to keep it just to have it.

I remember cracking the front bumper on a tree during the winter one year. I was working at National Bank and Trust in the branch at Coltonville Road (aka Rich Road). I loved working as a teller there. I hated having to leave, but I was so sick during my pregnancy that I just couldn't stay.

Anyway, I left work one winter evening and drove around the building to exit. The driveway around the side was curved in two places, one was nearly a 90* turn. I started sliding after the first curve and couldn't get control before it slid over the edge of the driveway, there was no curb, and into the tree. I was hardly moving so it only cracked the bumper but, in true Brent fashion, when I told him about it, he got very upset. Didn't ask how I was—maybe he assumed I was fine since he was looking at me? Not sure. It would have been nice to have him ask.

We also locked ourselves out of that apartment a couple times. The one time that sticks in my head was on Easter Sunday of '92 or '93. We were hustling out for church as it was always a struggle to get us all out the door on time. When we got to the cars, Brent and I realized neither of us had keys. We couldn't go anywhere and couldn't get back inside. Somehow we called Chris, one of our best friends, and he rescued us. He drove over with a ladder. We knew the front window—which was also the largest window—was unlocked. But, because we were on the second floor we couldn't get to it. He brought a ladder and used that to get to the window, popped the screen off and climbed through the window onto the sofa.

We had to warn him to be careful where he stepped as he climbed in the window. The Easter Bunny had arrived, but the kids had not been able to hunt for eggs in our haste to get to church. Eggs were on the couch and floor and we didn't want him to crack any. They were just plastic, but still.

One night I was folding clothes and went to the kids' room to hang them up and put them away. While in there, I could hear the kids ask Brent where Mommy was. He told them to go look for me. I heard them coming so I just stood still where I was. In plain sight next to the closet. They came in, looked around and left without seeing me. Grinning, I sat down on the floor so if they came in, we would be eye level with each other. They came in again, looked around and left without seeing me. I started quietly laughing as I didn't want to give away my position but it was so funny. They had literally looked right at me! It wasn't until the third time they came looking that they found me! We laughed about that for a long time.

They raised the rent in subsequent years to $580. Who knew we could afford that? Ha. But we did somehow.

The Parsonage

In August of 1994, we moved into the parsonage of Grace UMC in Maple Park. No, we were not suddenly ministers in the Methodist church. The appointed minister was not interested in moving into the parsonage. He was a professor at NIU in DeKalb and had no intention of moving into the little tiny town he would now be shepherding half the citizens of.

That was a boon for us. We were still in the 2-bedroom, 1-bathroom apartment on Stonehenge in Sycamore with three children under 5. Tony was of age to start kindergarten that fall and the idea of sending him to Kaneland was appealing. The rent was only about $100 more than our apartment and so much more space. The parsonage was a 3 bedroom, 1 bath ranch on the corner of Elm and Liberty. It had a 2-car garage attached and extra storage, a fenced in backyard and a sun porch. So much extra space.

Two weeks before we got the news of approval to rent the parsonage, Tony came down with the chicken pox. Smack in the middle of summer he wakes up one morning with small red spots spreading across his torso.

My mother quickly confirmed it was chicken pox and advised that we get Norah and Jodi exposed so all can have it and be done. Of course, I feared getting it myself since I had not had the disease. We also feared infecting unsuspecting people at a friend's wedding early in August. But, after explaining the situation to the bride, she told us to come on up. I'm sure it would have messed up their plans because Tony was ringbearer and I think Brent was in the wedding.

We went to the wedding and had a wonderful, fun weekend bar hopping in Wisconsin and celebrating our friends' marriage. At this point I was a stay-at-home mom so I looked for any excuse to get dressed up. I was wearing dressy clothes, heels, the whole nine yards. Then we walked around to so many bars on the night of the rehearsal. The next day I wore heels again for the wedding and the reception. We had a very fun time but my back and legs were killing me. They were used to flats and running shoes, not pinchy, but super cute, heels.

On the Monday after the wedding, I invited Aunt Gloria to come over and help me pack. Or at least help me wrangle the kids so I could get some time to pack. We only had 2 weeks to move out and clean the apartment to turn back over to the landlord. Not much time when you have 3 children. Little did I know that the time would be shortened even more because I had the chicken pox.

As I stood in front of the hall closet debating where to start with the sorting, I rubbed my hand up my arm and noticed a bump on the back of it. I immediately showed it to Aunt Gloria who confirmed, once again, chicken pox. I knew I was in a race against the disease at that point. I rushed to pack everything I possibly could in that house before I was too sick to help.

In 5 days' time, I packed that house up as much as I could. When our friends and family arrived on Saturday morning it was all pretty much packed and I was delirious with illness. To this day I don't remember large chunks of that weekend of moving. I know we had several people with trucks and trailers helping. I remember being put to bed on a pallet of blankets and pillows laid on the floor of the dining room while my bed was being made up. We had a waterbed at the time so the bed had to be assembled, filled and heated before I could get in. That was an all-day affair. I remember my mom filling the bathtub with warm water and oatmeal and making me get in. It felt so good though. I don't know why I resisted.

That oatmeal is a wonder when it comes to relieving itching. I know my mother-in-law set up my kitchen as a help. I do greatly appreciate her efforts in that. But it took me some time to find things and get them where I wanted them. In the end, it was truly by the efforts of family and friends that we got moved in that weekend.

I asked my grandma to help clean out the apartment in order to get it in condition to return to the landlord. I knew she would do a great job and she did. Spic and span it was. But, as corporate landlords do, they wanted to fine us for a soap ring in the tub among other things. I knew darn well my grandmother would not leave a soap ring in the tub. I refused to pay. We negotiated an agreement where we didn't pay but we also didn't get our security deposit back. That was highly disappointing but solidified my resolve to not rent from a corporate landlord again.

During our time living in the parsonage, many family milestones were met. Tony started kindergarten that fall and Norah the year after. I went to work shortly after Tony started school. We found a sitter who did daycare in her home and was reasonably priced. She had a boy the same age as Jodi so that would give her someone to play with. Norah was the oldest by quite a bit, but I think that worked for Norah. She was kind of a helper to Angie.

I started working at the bank—Old Second National Bank in Maple Park. My first job was in the mortgage servicing department and my job was to reconcile PMI payments on all loans that required PMI. Each morning I would arrive to binders full of dot matrix reports listing the loans and payments. I would sort through all the reports and confirm payments were made.

My desk was a 6-foot folding table with a folding chair. My office supplies consisted of a push button desk phone, a couple pens, highlighters and a ruler to keep my lines straight when viewing the reports. A very tedious job it was, but it started me in mortgages, a career that has served me well overall.

While we lived in the Parsonage, our two closest friends, Chris and Teddy, decided to get married—finally! They had been dating since high school, 5 years now. They had been so helpful and the most accepting of all our friends with the kids. They didn't leave us to our own devices.

However, there was one moment when Teddy pulled me aside that was a bit difficult. We were just hanging out at the house, kids playing outside, Brent and Chris shooting the breeze. Teddy followed me out to the garage and said she wanted to talk to me about something. I could tell she was anxious about what she had to say but had no clue what it would be about.

I can still see the garage behind her: the plywood shelves along the side wall with various boxes and cartons piled to the ceiling. Many, if not all of these things, are no longer with me today. The cars were not in the garage for some reason, they were on the driveway. Maybe the kids had been riding their bikes in the garage—if the weather was dicey we would do that sometimes.

She brought up the wedding and said she wanted to tell me something that Chris had said. They were talking about the wedding party and who would be their best man and maid of honor. I did not get my hopes up as Teddy had 3 sisters, so no shot. What she did say was that Chris felt Brent was his best friend but was uncertain about asking him for that role. His reasoning was the strained relationship Brent and I had at times. Specifically, how Brent would treat me. He didn't want to say anything directly to Brent necessarily, but he wanted him to know that if Brent was going to be in his wedding, he would need to take steps towards improving our relationship.

Well you could have knocked me over with a feather when she said this to me. I knew that sometimes he would say or do things I didn't like but I didn't realize how much it was obvious to and affecting others. Looking back now, it's a little embarrassing that I stayed in the marriage as long as I did. But I also knew at the time that I was doing what I thought was best. After all, marriage is to be until death. The problem is, what death? Not just the death of a spouse, but death of love, honor, respect, even just simply caring for your spouse.

After that conversation, I thought long and hard about what she said. Was I being mistreated? Should I be demanded more respect from him? Was it worth the struggle, energy, tension? Eventually, late one night while lying in bed, I did broach the subject with him. I told him straight up what Teddy said.

Chris doesn't want you for his best man unless you make some changes in how you treat me. Word for word, what she said. I don't remember a big blow up or response. I remember that we talked it through, he wanted to know more about what things Chris was referring to. I don't remember him asking me how I felt about how I was treated, which now I think is interesting. That is typical narcissistic behavior, to think about what he has to do to get to the goal or reward. Not to think about how he deals with people in his way. Now I know that.

That conversation was the catalyst for going back to our marriage counselor. We had started seeing her when I was pregnant with Jodi. That pregnancy was very difficult for some reason. I was nearly always nauseous and rarely felt good.

I worked until I was about 7 months along, maybe only 6. I loved that job as a bank teller. But my co-worker wore a very strong perfume. I think it was Tabu. She was a great lady, loved working with her. But she was constantly spraying perfume on herself because she would take smoke breaks. After each break, she would spray it again. That perfume made me feel so ill. We worked the drive-up window for The National Bank & Trust Co of Sycamore's Coltonville branch. I had regulars I got to see often and yet was insulated from the public too. It was the perfect job for an introvert. It was low stress. Everything was done during the day, nothing to take home and worry about. It was the perfect job for a busy mom of 2, going on 3, children.

The reason we went to the counselor was largely because Brent was upset with me for always feeling sick and even thought I was faking it. Why I would do that with pregnancy number 3 and not with the first or second is anyone's guess. That said, we found an older lady in St. Charles and visited her several times to work out some differences. I think some issues were helped, but I do think some issues were not. I also think that our time with her helped with our communication with each other, but I learned over the years that it never truly stuck. We'd be fine as long as we were in constantly counseling. But, about a week or two later, maybe a month if it was really good work, we'd be right back at it again.

Over the years we went to several different counselors to get us through difficult times. Looking back, it feels like those difficult times were always dictated by him. He decided that I needed to get help for something. Usually it was about our sex life. I could never give him enough sex. I swear, even if we had sex daily it wasn't enough. Like seriously? How is that not enough? For me, sex isn't such an earthshattering moment. Don't get me wrong, sex, when done right, feels incredible. But, in order to do it right, one must be extremely vulnerable with one's partner. And that is the core of the problem.

I know now, 25+ years later, that I didn't trust Brent fully and completely during our marriage. Even before to be honest. There was a time when I was out of town on a Girl Scout trip when we were seniors that I found out he went out with another girl. And then there was a time when I was pregnant that we got into an argument at my house and he stormed out of there angry and drove his car insanely down Mt. Hunger as I watched him. I feared he would hurt himself or possibly never come back. As a 16- or 17-year-old girl, it's scary to have that happen. Which, if he hadn't come back, may have been for the best.

But it is my past, my story. Those events and moments all come together to make me the person I am today. To make my children the people they are today. To make my ex the person he is today. I think we would all agree we are pretty good people today and in a good place mentally. My children all lead productive happy lives and have healthy relationships with their chosen mates. Their children are happy, thriving children. I am blessed beyond measure.

We bought our first every brand-new furniture from a retail store when we lived in the parsonage. It was a set of bunkbeds and 2 dressers which I still have. They were wooden bunkbeds with slats to hold the mattresses. The dressers were relatively small, but the girls were about 5 and 3 when we bought them so the size worked for their little clothes.

I have a picture of them proudly sitting in their beds after we put them up. They were so excited. Norah with her little short haircut Mom had given her. The moment that changed the course of their relationship forever. And Jodi just grinning because she was included with her sister. That was always her favorite. To be included with her sister.

Of course, Norah would sometimes take advantage of being the big sister. Like she would have Jodi come ask for something that she wanted. I guess she thought we couldn't say no. One of my favorite memories is when we went to McDonald's for dinner one night. Jodi would have been about 3, making Norah about 5 or 6. Each of the kids had their happy meal. I'm pretty sure Norah had a cheeseburger. But she needed ketchup.

I'm sure we had some, but it most likely wasn't enough. Norah loved ketchup, she would dip anything and everything in ketchup. She dipped green beans, and once did peaches because her Aunt Rosie bribed her with funny money. So, at McDonald's this night, she needed more ketchup but was too shy to go to the counter to get it from the server. She ended up taking Jodi with her. As we watched them, we realized that Jodi was the one who asked for and received the ketchup, immediately giving it to her sister. We still tease Norah with that story today. It will be interesting to see if her twins do similar actions.

We implemented a "snack administrator" program with the kids. We got tired of them asking all the time for snacks. So sometimes, the kids were the snack administrators so they got to choose who got what and when. Usually this was on a weekend day that we were home most of the day, but I think it was a great way to show them some independence as well as decision making skills. We didn't do it for those reasons, but that was definitely a good byproduct. So many of our parenting decisions had unintended consequences that were usually positive for us.

We were so blessed that way. Although, I do remember when Tony was a baby, an infant, we discussed that we wanted our kids to behave in public. We were at a restaurant eating dinner. Tony was in his little kanga-rock-a-roo seat on the table.

There was a little boy in the booth next to us who kept popping up and interrupting us. He was trying to talk to us and would be constantly interrupting. As we worked our way through that dinner, we made the decision to have our children behave in public if not any other time. I'd say it worked out well.

We also expected them to care for one another and stand up for one another. There was not fighting with each other like I've heard about in so many families. Sure, they argued some but it wasn't knock-down, drag-out fighting or nasty name calling like I've heard of in so many families. Through the years I realize how blessed we are with the children loving each other and caring for each other in such a way.

Of course, their parents did plenty of fighting so maybe that's why they didn't... I don't know.

Housekeeping

I've never been one with a worry about housekeeping. I received a poem from someone when Tony was born that said:

"Cleaning and scrubbing can wait til tomorrow for babies grow up we've learned to our sorrow. So quiet down cobwebs, dust go to sleep. I'm rocking my baby and babies don't keep."

That poem has been my life's mantra really when it came to choosing family time or cleaning. I feel like I'm better than my mom was, but my kids are definitely better than I was at housekeeping. During my visit with Jodi, she tells me that her and Norah would like me to do the "Marie Kondo" thing to my place. Well, I really think I do pretty good but she says it's the clutter.

Well, yes, I will concede clutter is an issue for me.

The irony is that I was just thinking about how my kids are much better at keeping house than I was and I'm so glad for them. I like a nice neat and tidy home but I can't seem to keep it that way. This afternoon I sent a text to Norah and told her that if she truly wanted to help me with this, I'd be more than happy to accept it. No answer yet, but in fairness, I think she's at work.

Brent was never fastidious about housekeeping either. I'm pretty sure he always viewed that as my job. Just like he did the cooking, the bulk of the children's disciplines and decisions. Yet he would feel compelled to put in his two cents even when I wasn't asking for it. I also knew that if I didn't follow his recommendation, he would be sure to remind me if my plan failed. And gloat if his plan was successful. He would make fun of my mother for her piles of magazines and papers.

While I understand that, because she is the master at stacking things of that nature, making fun of someone, especially if that someone is your wife's mom, isn't the most flattering of actions. I do remember trying to straighten things up from time to time. He usually failed to help. But, if someone was coming to visit, then he'd be on the ball about it. So much so that it would drive me nuts. Just super intense. And things had to be perfect when we had a visitor. It was really quite exhausting because keeping the house clean, working full time and putting up a façade of the "perfect family" are all quite hard to manage at one time.

He would make comments like, "We live in a shithole". His passive aggressive way of telling me I wasn't keeping up with the house, laundry, etc. After years of this, I finally decided to let the outdoor chores go. I love to garden—vegetables and flowers. But something had to give as I realized I couldn't do it all. Then he started griping because I never helped him in the yard. This was about 15 years into our marriage.

After 15 years of trying to keep up, actually 16 if you count the time we lived together before marrying, I just knew it wasn't gonna happen. I started ignoring his comments about my lack of help with the outdoor chores. Never mind that I was the only one cooking dinner each night. Never mind that I was the only one focusing on laundry even though I had asked repeatedly for assistance with it. Sure he would help, for a few days at most and then fall off again. His job was always ok for him to spend a million hours a week on, but not me.

It was a mirror for how lopsided our relationship was. I did the work and he would come in and collect the reward, soak up the praise, enjoy the moment. To be fair, I'm sure he would say the same thing about me because from his perspective, it may have felt that way, but maybe fill in different things—like he would be the one to say he did all the yard work and grilling out while I sat in the house watching T.V. or playing with the kids or doing crafts. Certainly not working hard. But this book is about my perspective, not his.

He would say he took the lead in our relationship too. Which, he would mean, he took the lead in our physical relationship. After a time, I just gave up and let him do as he wished. I was not excited about sex with him and did not want to have it. But, as a wife, there are certain duties you perform, right? At least, that's what I told myself. Our counselor called it "mercy fucking". I completely related to that term. That's exactly what I was doing, but even after the counselor identified it and he understood what that meant, he continued to demand more physical intimacy. The problem is, that's like demanding respect, it's just not how that works.

Physical intimacy requires trust. I'm not sure I ever trusted my husband beyond the first few years. But that trust was definitely broken when, one Easter morning, he revealed to me that he had cheated on me. He told me how he was at a work conference and the office admin was there with him, as well as 2 or 3 co-workers. His story went like this:

One night they all were at the bar, he was drinking too much and she was too. He was concerned about her and helped her to her room. (See how he makes it about how good of a person he is?) When she was in the room, she went into the bathroom and he waited to make sure she got back out and was safely tucked into bed. But, she didn't come out, she had tried to take a shower or bath and ended up naked. He couldn't resist himself. He says there was never actual intercourse, but I don't know that it really matters. The fact he would go that far anyway was too much for me.

As for the cheating, my reaction to it was complete and total shock that quickly dissolved into total grief. I couldn't understand it at all. Why would he jeopardize our life this way? For a little quickie? It made me wonder if he really did only that. But he never admitted to more and I don't think it matters. The damage to the relationship was done.

I always felt that he was too dominating in bed and other aspects of our relationship. That's the reason I did not like sex necessarily. It was his way or the highway, just like the rest of our marriage. As a sexual molestation survivor, that's probably the worst thing you can do to someone: not let them have control of their own body.

Since my marriage ended and I dated other men, had relationships with other men, and subsequently married my amazing husband, I have come to find out it's not sex that I don't like. It's the emotional factors that surrounded the sex in my first marriage that I didn't like.

Looking back at this time, I can see that was the true beginning of the end of our marriage. Don't get me wrong, I fought like hell to keep it together. I did journaling, prayer, meditation. I suggested dates and tried to spend time with him doing things he enjoyed. We went to a counselor again, this time a man as I thought maybe he could relate better to Brent and really help us dig into the truest issues. I took a personal retreat a couple years later to evaluate my thoughts on the marriage.

During that retreat, I rededicated myself to keeping the marriage together. I read books on how to reinforce your marriage after an episode like this. I talked with Brent about these ideas and techniques. But a marriage just cannot be saved alone. It takes two to make it work. Brent had started to check out also by this time.

I look at my journals from this time and there are budgets based on my income to see if I could afford to live separately. There are calculations for child support. Listing of debts and assets and how they could be split. It wasn't until I read through my journals for the project of this book that I realized I did these things at this time. I thought it was much later before I seriously thought of divorce. I realize now that I was starting to value myself in a way that my husband never would.

Maybe it was all the prayer, journaling, meditating that brought this to me, but I know I was looking at myself as a stronger person than before the infidelity happened. I knew what it was now to be confronted by such a horrible abuse of trust and to survive it. The saying "what doesn't kill you makes you stronger" is very true. By becoming stronger, I learned to be more proactive in asserting my needs, not just trying to meet everyone else's. I started doing things on my own instead of frustrating myself by trying to get Brent to come along. I started reading again no matter what comments I might receive. Taking back that little bit of control was vital to me becoming the person I am today.

The Grand Palm

The anxiety of the summer of 2010.

Not knowing where your children will sleep in the near future drives anxiety sky high. The unsettled feelings of how I'm going to provide shelter for them dominate my days and torment my nights. A constant feeling of unease and uncertainty follows me through all my movements.

After a rocky spring of losing a job, getting a job, losing a job, finally admitting to the need for filing bankruptcy, losing a car to repossession, filing said bankruptcy and all the while knowing you cannot afford to live in your home anymore, I am exhausted emotionally.

For the past few weeks, I've been working at home for a mortgage loan processing company as a contract processor. The problem is that there is not enough work to keep me busy or to pay the bills. I've been working in the upstairs office with the windows open to avoid turning on the AC. Everything is covered with pollen daily and I find myself cleaning the space each morning. But, by noon, my hands have that rough feeling that announces I'm covered in pollen once again. I'm sure this is not good for my computer and printer. And the humidity in Georgia doesn't help either.

But, here I sit, looking out the window at my kids playing basketball on the driveway. Wondering, where we will live when the bank forecloses. Will we even be able to rent a place large enough for 2 adults, 4 nearly grown children and 2 dogs? How much is that going to cost, how much for a pet deposit? The only reason we got the dogs 6 years ago was because we bought the house. But now we will lose it. It's just a matter of time.

We have had some rough times financially, but never have I ever worried that my children would have no place to lay their heads at night. I'm not even thinking about safety or comfort. Just a basic roof over their heads.

So much uncertainty. Some might say fix up your house and sell it. The market is so bad right now, and we have leveraged all we could in the preceding years to make improvements, we are now upside by quite a bit. We have requested a modification based on my income drop and job losses. But this process was started months ago, and who knows if or when we will get that relief.

I shudder to think what my credit score must look like right now. It is surely at the bottom of the barrel. This will add to the difficulty in getting a rental home as most landlords want good credit—understandably so. Which means an apartment is the next best option, and I hate having corporate landlords. Every time I have had a corporate landlord, they have charged me stupid amounts for made up repairs and cleaning after I've moved out. It's a racket.

This brings me back to the issue, the reason for my many sleepless nights and untold anxiety.

Modification package was returned again for more documentation. I'm not sure why they keep sending the entire package back. It's obnoxious. And then we have to start over at the end of the line again.

Collecting paperwork to document our loss of income over the last couple of years and crafting letters of explanation about these circumstances are the reason for my existence these days. It's probably a good thing I don't have any loans to process since I doubt I could focus on them anyway.

W2 forms, tax return documents, verifications of employment, letters explaining dates of employment, salary amounts, benefits allowed and accepted are stuffed in this envelope. Yet somehow it's still not enough information to determine that we can't make our payment. I guess I need to actually make a late payment for them to realize we are seriously in trouble here. Although, I would think that the bankruptcy and car repossession would be clues enough. Maybe they think we can make the payments easily now because we don't have those payments? I don't know what else they could be thinking.

After several months, we finally got the modification, although it didn't change the payment nearly as much as we had hoped. I had been out of work now for some time. And that was after months, if not years, of being paid less than I had previously been making.

The thing is, God's timing is always the best. Even though many times it feels like He's not paying any attention to your life and needs, He really does have your best life in His hands. I look back at that summer and realize that even though it was heavy with worry and anxiety, I learned that summer to really give my worries and cares over to God continually.

Now, I do not always hand everything over to Him like I should. But this was the summer I learned how much that actually works and changes life if you allow it to. The key: you must choose this. Choose to hand over your concerns because quite honestly, God's got a plan for you and if you get out of His way, it will all work out in the end. No endless amount of worry will alter His plans but by acting outside of His best for you and acting before it is the right time, you can alter your life.

What's your biggest issue right now? That thing that is there in the front of your mind right now as you try to read this book. What is it? Name it. Journal about it, pray over it, ask God for His guidance, and then GIVE IT TO HIM. I have in the past, many times, made the motion of handing over my worries to God. Physically moving my hands upward and outward while opening my fists to a flat palm. This is an action we would take to hand an item over to another person. Use this action, this physical movement, to truly give it over to Him. He has everything worked out and in the end, you'll feel silly for all the time, energy, and embarrassing actions you took while stressing yourself out over the issue. It's just that simple. Yet so very, very difficult.

Teens

Many years after becoming a mom, I finally realized what a true gift it was. This summer, the one so filled with anxiety and worry and concern, gave me time to bond with my kids and learn who they were in a way I never realized was so vitally important.

Not to say I didn't have flashes of mom feelings many many times throughout my life, but it wasn't until this summer when I was home with my all teenage crew that I realized life was beautiful. Even in the midst of the anxiety and worry about the house and the finances, this was probably some of the best bonding times I'd had with my kids. I think these may have been the times when I stumbled upon developing the relationships that I now enjoy tremendously with my kids. They all are unique, loving individuals who make such an impact in their circles of influence.

I'm incredibly proud of how they all turned out and I truly believe it has to do with being real, admitting my mistakes to them as needed, but also, giving their lives to God as often as I could remember to do so. I still pray for them and their families (future and present) and will do so for the rest of my life. I may not remember everyone's birthdays like my grandmother did until her dying day, but I will remember the love, the joy, the beauty of life with them.

A quick story about my youngest and his independence.

Peter has always had the heart of an entrepreneur and made that clearly known before middle school. He tried multiple times with friends to start a lawn-mowing business. They never really got off the ground. But he had other successful ventures.

When Peter was in middle school, I noticed that we were going through a lot of gum as a family. I found this to be strange since at least 2 of my kids were in braces at the time and I was pretty particular about them not chewing gum. Let's be honest though, I'm sure they did some. That said, I still had a big gum shortage happening and didn't know why. One night at dinner, one of the kids comments to Peter about his business and how it was going. He tries to hush up the conversation, which is all the more reason why I would not let the conversation end.

Asking the other kids to explain further what they were talking about, I discovered that Peter has been selling gum on the bus. Gum that he was taking from our kitchen drawer. That was apparently the source of the gum shortage. Peter has gone on to become quite the entrepreneur. He recently sold his first business and is starting up a second one. That business was built while working full time as a restaurant manager and a realtor.

Can You See It?

Shortly after one of my parents' visits, my mom and I had talked about my concerns over my relationship with Brent and she suggested that I not engage with him when he was being unreasonable or difficult. I remember feeling like that was such a great idea and wondering how I hadn't thought of it before! I committed to myself to try this approach, especially when others were around, to lessen our friction and hopefully improve our times together.

There were times that I would think Brent was just picking at me for no reason. Actually, it felt like most times. I was thinking if only one of his relatives—his brother or sister-in-law or cousin could see this behavior— maybe they could explain it to him in a way that would get him to stop.

Once when JuJu was visiting, I was starting to feel that Brent was constantly picking at me. I remember standing in my kitchen making dinner with JuJu there chatting. It was a gorgeous sunshiny Georgia day. Brent was outside on the deck. He came through the kitchen and while doing so, made a snarky comment to me. I forget now what he said, but I know that on this occasion I had said nothing to him.

I had learned some time ago to not even reply when he did that. Reacting to him never produced anything good, it would just spiral downward. I looked at his cousin and asked, "Was that me? Did I say something to him to deserve that?" She, who never inserts herself into family squabbles, said, "I understand what you mean now." That validated me.

At this point my emotions were dying, on their last breath. I was really just looking to confirm I wasn't crazy in thinking I hadn't done anything to deserve the snarkiness. Prior incidents had left me feeling inferior in some way, stupid or irrational. Just trying to defuse the situation even though I didn't know what the situation was. This kind of abuse had been happening for years and as far as I could see, would continue to happen until and unless I personally separated myself from the situation.

Becoming Stronger

Learning to stand up for yourself is a very scary proposition when you've spent years and years being pushed down. Especially when you still have not realized that you have been pushed down and made to feel inferior. How can you see your own value when you see yourself through the eyes of someone who constantly finds fault with what you do and how you do it?

Motherhood has a way of making us doubt ourselves and our abilities. Nothing in life challenges us like a child does with their own ways and ideas. As a young mother, I struggled with my identity and valuing what I had to give to my children. What could I, as a teenage mom, a screw-up, a failure, have to offer these kids other than getting them through each day safely, fed and with shelter? My self-worth dropped to an all-time low during these beginning years of motherhood.

As my life went, these years also coincided with the beginning years of my marriage. Did this lack of self-worth influence my marriage? Surely it did. Brent thought he was getting a fun-loving, vivacious, teen girl as his bride when inside I was a scared little girl with no confidence and even less self-worth. That is not a good way to start any relationship, and least of all one of the most influential relationships of your life.

Through the years, I gained confidence when I would excel at work or in my home duties in some way. I know cooking was a great source of pride. I fed my family well—sometimes I made mistakes, like the cream of broccoli soup incident—but overall, they were well fed. I'm a good cook. I know this now after 20+ years of cooking for a crew of 6. But now, in my empty nester life, cooking is not a vital skill the same way as it was when the kids were all at home.

I kept striving for the right way to live my life. I learned that God needed to be the center. He is the source of confidence and His presence makes our life on earth worthwhile. If we can help each other on this earth, we can be assured of doing His work.

Gaining confidence in myself was developed largely by studying the Bible, journaling and surrounding myself with women who were already through the trials I was experiencing.

God put the right people in my path, even when I didn't know they were the right people. I had a great boss who I'm still friends with to this day. He helped me see the value of myself simply by trusting me to do my job and to run the office when he was not there.

That relationship taught me that we all—bankers, CEOs, janitors and loan processors—put our pants on one leg at a time. No one is greater than or lesser than anyone else unless they choose to be treated that way.

As Eleanor Roosevelt once said, "No one can make you feel inferior without your consent." Choose to live your life as a worthy, valuable, person. Don't be superior, but don't be inferior either.

Chapter 4

Transitioning

Through the years, Brent and I had tried many different options for additional income. One of those options was to become Amway distributors. During our tenure, we found ourselves making trips for conferences. We took our baby girl with us to Miami for a conference when she was only 2 weeks old. It was the first time I had been to Miami, maybe Brent too, I honestly do not know. Miami is a very interesting city. The architecture is unique in a way that is all South Beach.

Another one of the trips sent us to Atlanta in the spring of 1993 when they had a huge blizzard across the southeast. It made for quite a mess in the city with not enough equipment for clearing the snow. We stayed a day or two extra but then decided to trek home. It was quite a challenge to make our way through the icy and slippery interstates across the south, still covered in snow even days later. It took about 24 hours for us to get from Atlanta to Chicago. We ended up driving so far west and when we realized we wouldn't outdrive the snow that way, we finally turned north.

A third trip was to Bristol, Tennessee. Bristol is an interesting city because it sits on the border of Tennessee and Virginia. This is quite beautiful country. We spent time in the Cherokee National Forest. Climbed to the top of a hill that felt like we were climbing up a mountain. But it was so beautiful, I really didn't mind at all. We stood in that very park and determined that we needed to move our family south. We loved Bristol but knew it could prove foolish to narrow our options to such a small geographic area. I feel that might have been one of the times we were truly in sync during our marriage, when we were planning to move south.

We had a lot of conversations about where we would want to go. Of course, the first step was getting a job in an area we wanted to live in. Brent had been working in sales for a bit by this time, computer sales.

We started looking for jobs in the south, anywhere really. We also looked at jobs that were in the north with the possibility of relocating to the south. We had a combined purpose and goal. We found ourselves to be quite happy about how we worked together, each using our strengths to manage this process.

A few months later he got a call from one of the online companies that was expanding into new markets and looking to hire sales and territory managers for these new markets. Eventually he was offered the position and he started working for them in their Chicagoland office.

After just a few months, he was offered a new market location, Minneapolis. Uh, no thank you. Shortly after that, they offered Boston. I don't think so. We want to go south, but if not south, to somewhere we can comfortably raise our family. The third offer was much more aligned to our plans: Charlotte, North Carolina. Yes, indeed, yes! We were so excited about this prospect!

We immediately called our realtor to start working on the house sale. The kids were out of school for the summer so we put them to work sorting their rooms, toys, and such. Getting rid of anything they felt they should get rid of. It's really quite therapeutic to shed excess belongings.

By Labor Day, the house was sold. Brent had been in North Carolina for a few weeks already and had found a house for us to rent. The kids and I stayed for the final 3 weeks in Illinois in my grandparents' RV at my parents' house. School had not started in Illinois yet but had started in Charlotte 3 weeks earlier, so we had some informal homeschooling.

My dad took on the science course by spending time with the kids outside teaching them to identify the kinds of trees, flowers, and the like. Mom had the kids help with harvesting from the garden. My aunt, an elementary school teacher, provided math worksheets for the kids to use.

It was a fun 3 weeks really. The kids were able to experience much of my childhood: playing with kittens, working in the vegetable garden, picking delicious fruits and eating them while standing in the warm sunshine. It's really the most delightful way to eat fresh fruits and vegetables.

On Labor Day weekend, we packed up the rental truck and put the van on the trailer behind it. A large party with friends and family—so many people because we invited anyone we had known. We all hung out for the entire day together. Some people popped in and left again, but most people stayed for the entire time. I kissed all the babies, played with all the children, had my share of libations and generally enjoyed the day.

The next morning came quickly as we were up before the sun to get on the road. Three kids and I drove in the Olds 88 while Brent and 1 kid drove the truck. They were all to take turns going from the car to the truck. We had walkie talkies to use to communicate with each other too.

This was before cell phones were in everyone's hands so this was a plan we came up with to make everyone happy. The kids were so excited about our new adventure but I think at this point it was the road trip to a new place they were most excited about. Of course, there had been many tears over the last couple of days as we said our goodbyes to so many. And now it felt good to be happy, excited and looking forward again.

We had estimated the drive to take about 12 hours. However, at some point while in the mountains, we were detoured off the interstate on to tight, winding mountains roads with semis all around. It made me rather nervous but we had no plans to stop anywhere overnight so we had to charge on. After what seemed like hours and when it felt like it was in the middle of the night, we finally made it out to an interstate again. By now, I was just flat out exhausted. We had been on the road for 18 hours straight. I radioed up to talk to Brent and tell him I needed a break.

We ended up pulling over on the side of the highway. The kids were all sleeping, Brent and I met at the back of the truck and I proceeded to just melt down. Completely past my wits. He might even say I was hysterical. And, when looking at the strict definition (deriving from uncontrolled extreme emotion), it fits. I have to admit, I was inconsolable. I was so worn out I couldn't think straight. I told Brent that I was not getting back in the car, that I was not going to be able to finish this drive.

I was adamant. I think the best thing he did that day was listen to me. I'm not sure if he listened quietly or just truly did not know what to say. I finally settled down enough to be persuaded to get back in the car and drive on.

We arrived at the hotel where Brent had been staying for the past three weeks. I don't know what we were thinking to have the idea of all 6 of us staying in one small hotel room. After 20 hours driving in the car after a very emotional send-off from family and friends, finding the hotel was a true excitement for us. The kids were wound up from lack of exercise and the thrill of being in a hotel. It took quite a while to get them all settled and figure out who would sleep where. Finally, we all settled and slept, even if it was fitfully.

The next morning, we all went out to breakfast and then drove the truck to the new house. It was the first time I saw it and I was a bit let down. The kitchen had vinyl flooring with a brick pattern and an olive-green refrigerator.

The majority of the house was covered in brown shag carpet. That was a bit much but it was nice since it wouldn't show when it was dirty. We toured the 3-bedroom, 2-bath ranch quickly. No garage or basement, but the backyard had a dirt bike path of sorts that the kids used quite a bit.

I stood in the sad little kitchen feeling somewhat let down. The home we had in Illinois was much prettier, larger, brighter. But there I was. What to do now? While standing there in the quiet, I distinctly heard the Lord's voice speaking to me. He simply said, this won't be for long. I didn't know what he meant, but I took comfort in it. At the very least what I did know was that God was right there with me. That was enough to get me started on unloading the truck and commencing our time in Charlotte, however long it was to end up being.

I am gay.

Those three little words rocked my world. My then-15-year-old cousin, a sweet teenager who I had known from before she was born, told me this. All I could feel was an incredibly heavy sadness for her. The life she was choosing was going to be rife with struggle and fear. But I never even questioned my love for her. I would never throw her out on the street for this, that was inconceivable to me, even as I heard these words.

I am a Christian, was then and still am. As we all know, there are some teachings in the Bible that arguably state that homosexual relations are "abominable" to God. I am not going to get into a debate about gay lifestyle, but having this dear child say this to me made me think twice.

I know this child. Like I KNOW her. I was there at her birth, watching as her mother labored and worked and pushed to bring her forth in this world. I cared for her as an infant. As she grew, I watched her learn to explore, be curious, ask questions. As she became a young woman, I watched as she learned to listen to her body and to believe in her own convictions, to be strong in ways that weren't physical. Yet, she figured out the physical too. Such a strong, beautiful, intelligent, seeking, questioning, loving, compassionate young woman.

I remember when she was in about first grade and played basketball at our church. She had only been in the area for about 4 months and had not yet made many new friends, or so she thought.

Yet, when it came to the end of year awards ceremony, she won the most significant award. The one where all the coaches and facilitators came together and chose one boy and one girl out of all the first-to-fifth graders. The Christ-like award. This award went to the child who showed the most characteristics of Christ: love, compassion, empathy, etc. They announced the boy first. His family stood beaming, so happy for him. The audience applauded and cheered.

And then my sweet cousin was announced. The audience stood and hooted and hollered. They cheered like crazy! They started chanting her name over and over! It was the wildest thing!

I knew when she was born, looking down into her beautiful baby face, that she was destined for some amazing greatness far beyond anything I could imagine. In my humanity, I thought maybe she'd be the POTUS or another high-level politician and make real, lasting, effective change in the world. Maybe she'd be a missionary and go to places we'd never even heard of before. Maybe she'd do something that I couldn't even fathom because I am merely human. I felt this in my soul, in my heart, in my mind. I still feel this.

Still, knowing all this, I find my mind swirling with questions and emotions at her announcement. I know this child. I know her heart. She has a heart for God. She is more connected to God than anyone else I know.

Why would God allow this to be how she sees herself, what she feels and wants to live out, if it is so abominable to Him? He doesn't enjoy our suffering, his heart breaks when ours do. Yet, this was happening, it was really truly happening.

Don't get me wrong, I had suspected this for a while. The clothes she was wearing, the friends she had, or didn't, her lack of interest in boys as a 15-year-old girl. I remember talking to her mother about 4 months before her announcement about her clothing choices.

Not that I was going to make her wear something different, but so that she understood what the plaid button ups with jeans and minimal jewelry and boots were saying to the world. And, again, not to create a peer pressure situation, but to prepare her for people's remarks. She was choosing plaid flannel shirts, jeans, ball caps, things one would look on as stereotypical lesbian clothing choices.

After her revelation, my sweet niece seemed to be lighter and happier than she had been in months. Her mother told us that she ended up spending more time with the family than she had in months after sharing her announcement. Clearly, she had been feeling immense pressure about telling her family. If it means more family time, then maybe this is all worth it. The next morning, my first thought upon waking was, "The world did not end and God is still on His throne!"

For the next 5 years I wrestled with this announcement. How could my God, a God of love, allow His child, to be gay—something He hates? This didn't make sense when I rationalized it with who I know this child to be and who I know my God to be. For 5 years I studied, researched and explored the possibilities of what this lifestyle really meant to God and the world. I needed to know how she was going to be accepted in this world, what pitfalls to help her watch out for. Help her learn how to protect herself in this subsector of society that I personally knew nothing at all about.

My views on homosexuality were challenged, not just my faith. I thought it was an abomination too, because that's what I thought God's message had been. I was challenged with accepting the sinner, but not the sin. With loving the sinner and hating the sin.

I thought at first, maybe that's the lesson in it for me. I worked hard to accept everything my cousin was telling me. I asked questions when I had them; I encouraged her to focus on her schoolwork and other activities first, and not to concern herself with relationships for now. It's too distracting, when your goals are so huge, to be in a relationship and all the energy it takes to be emotionally invested with someone will take away from the energy you need for your goals.

As I worked through all of the emotions and challenges I felt during those 5 years, one of the thoughts I had about how to get to the bottom of the question of whether or not it is sin to act as a homosexual was to study Greek and Hebrew. If I studied those languages, I could then read the Bible in its original writings and determine for myself if God really said what is attributed to him. While trying to find places to learn this and to study the Bible in its original form, I continued to study, to read, and to pray.

I finally came to the conclusion that people are born as homosexuals. It was the only way it made sense to me at that time. I struggled with the modern interpretations of the Bible that said God abhors homosexuality. My cousin loves God and would not purposely sin against him in such an obvious way. Therefore, since this is not a choice, it must be simply the way she was made. Why else would this girl choose a life that is sinful and hard and painful? And, if it is a choice, why would God make someone that way, knowing those desires and feelings would lead to sin in His eyes?

During the 5 years I wrestled with this proclamation, I concluded that God is always loving, always knowing and truly does work all things together for good. I also confirmed that the world is going to do what it is going to do and say no matter what the Lord's counsel is on any given subject. The world is going to see things without the lens of the Lord. I also understood that some of the people who profess to be Christians think it's best to push their agenda just as hard as the LGBTQ community pushes theirs. It makes me think about the adage of the Old Testament which is an eye for an eye.

As time went on, my cousin continued to mature and explore the world around her. She graduated from high school and went away to college. During that time, her parents divorced. She tested relationships of her own. Eventually, she came to date a young man she had met and the two fell quickly and completely in love.

After talking with her about this man, I knew without a shadow of a doubt that she was indeed in love. Today, she is married to this young man and so very happy in her life as a mom. She is doing the "work" she is currently destined to be doing. And, some day when the kids are all grown and life changes again, she'll have that same loving, compassionate nature she is so well-known for and can choose to further her impact at that time.

My Step-Daughter

I first met my step-daughter in the fall of 2016. A sweet young lady with a cute pixie cut and troubled eyes.

I don't understand transgender. I just don't understand it and I don't know what to think about it. Why do you have to physically change who you are? There are research studies that show transgender people are no happier 30 years after their sex changes than they were before. And in some cases, they are actually more depressed and at a higher risk of suicide.

As far as I am aware, the Bible is silent on this type of transition or lifestyle. My theory? There is something that a transgender person just deep down doesn't like or doesn't understand about themselves. And they're just not equipped to figure it out, or maybe just don't want to. It's easier to just say I'm really someone different.

In the long run, I don't think it's easier. But most people do make these transgender decisions as teens, or even younger. A time when their physical bodies are still growing but even more importantly, when their brains are still developing. When their hearts and souls are not yet mature. Let's be honest, it's tough to figure yourself out, especially as a teen when things change on moment by moment and "the rest of your life" seems like an unimaginably long time. But to alter yourself chemically with hormone blockers and other pills, when there is nothing physically diseased, just seems like such a huge risk. How do you know that in 10 years you won't regret that?

When my cousin came to me about being gay, I was heartbroken for her living a life that I believed would have her sent to hell at the end of her earthly life. I thought, how does she know this at 15? But a friend asked me, "Didn't you know if you liked boys or not at 15?" I thought back to my teen years and agreed, yes, I did indeed know I liked boys. Of course, now I can see how that thinking is flawed, but it made sense at the time when I was desperately searching for something to help it all make sense.

What I did learn from my cousin is that life changes and sometimes you change too. Why did she announce her sexual orientation at 15 and then at 20 start dating a man whom she would eventually marry and have children with? My theory, as a very close relative, is that she was confused and hurting and this was a way to escape from what she saw as her future as a heterosexual. Do I think my step-daughter is similar this way? Yes, I think she is announcing her desire to be a boy in order to get some attention during an extremely tumultuous time in her life.

Do I think there are people who are born in the wrong body for their brain? It's entirely possible! The things we do, eat, chemicals we ingest—knowingly and unknowingly—can alter our physical makeup and end up corrupting certain genes which manifest as transgender.

In the end, each person has to make their own way, to write their own story if you will. Each story is unique, personal and beautiful in its own special ways.

The solution is to simply love each other as you would like to be loved. Love with patience, kindness and honor. Love that doesn't judge, that shows mercy, compassion, tolerance. And not just tolerance for people similar to myself (which is quite clearly the opposite of tolerance), but people who are quite different from me in all ways. Physically, spiritually, geographically, politically. All these ways are made to be so important in our world, but the differences we see in each other should be lauded as beauty and nurtured.

Becoming Kinder

The So That verse, 2 Corinthians 1: 3-4, tells us that God provides comfort to us and that we are to use that comfort to care for others. In verse 6, Paul goes on to tell us that if we ourselves are distressed or suffering, it is to help those with whom we interact. If we are helped, then so are those around us. We receive the patience to endure the same sufferings with each other. We should hope in one another again. Creating a world full of hope and kindness should be our mission every day.

A colleague of mine once said her goal each day was to improve herself by 1%. Some days that means drinking 1% more water than she did the day before. Or maybe working out 1% longer or journaling 1% more in her diaries. The point is that if we each can just do 1% better each day, eventually, we can all become better together.

Kindness, just like meanness, has a ripple effect like water moving when something touches it. No matter if you throw a huge rock with a large plop or a butterfly flits to the surface of a still pond, the effect will continue outward until the edges of the pond. But the choice is ours as to how we affect that pond.

Do we bulldoze through, cutting down anything in our path—the weeds and the flowers? Or, do we carefully make a path, loving the weeds and the flowers? At one time, all flowers were considered weeds anyway. Maybe that person who just treated you abysmally is simply a weed needing some kindness, patience and love.

Chapter 5

Bad Feelings

I don't want to write the bad stuff. I know I'm skirting around the issues. I really want to get these things out but it's hard, maybe it would be easier to handwrite. I don't want to go back to those feelings again. I hate the way he could make me feel and I don't relish exploring those feelings and getting them out on paper for all the world to experience.

I buoy my courage by remembering that this is being done to hopefully help whoever is experiencing similar situations. You must know that YOU are worthy of being more, wanting more, expecting more. In order to get that message out, I'll need to experience these feelings again one last time.

A Life-Altering Decision

One day I went to the library and looked up books that talked about the psychological effects of divorce on kids. I looked up multiple books and read them standing right there between the racks. I found books that said staying with your husband is good and why. I found books that said separating is better and why.

But I finally found one book that was a compilation of interviews with adults whose parents actually did divorce and those whose parents should have divorced but didn't. Those adults of the divorced parents didn't have much to say negative really. They said they thought their lives improved for the most part. And, for the adult children of those parents who should have divorced, they said they wish their parents had divorced instead of staying together.

Reading these words from the people themselves led me to take one step closer to the actual divorce. I knew this would be okay.

What was better? To live as a couple arguing and creating a tense environment for the kids to live in or to live separately and pass the kids and fight between us over custody, child support, etc? Not too much choice there really. I never trusted that he would actually pay me child support and never thought I could come up with the money to pay an attorney.

The work I did for years of raising his kids, making his meals, cleaning his house, laundry, bill paying, trying to keep all our shit together. And at times, there was a lot of shit. But, I did it all for the kids to have a family with 2 parents. I believed it was the right thing to do.

Then, he cheated. He cheated on me after all the years I had given him of me. The best of me.

I tried for years to forgive him. To make the changes he needed me to make. To make our home an even better environment for him. But, in the end, I just wasn't right for him and I was finally able to admit it.

Late in the month of June, met Brent at his office to see the new design and then have a date night for the first time in probably years. I decided to use this time to tell him the conclusion I had come to. I was very nervous, my breath was shallow, my heart was racing, my anxiety was off the charts. I parked in the garage, not near his vehicle, I didn't want to walk out together knowing what I was going to say to him.

I entered the office with a serious trepidation. He met me at the front and was happy to see me. I remember him that day as being on top of the world. This was his happy place. I felt guilty that I was going to destroy that shortly, but I also knew it must be done.

He showed me around the office with all the upgrades and changes he had worked on for months with no raise or promotion even though I had repeatedly encouraged him to request one or both. He was proud of his work.

I knew this, but I also knew I was checked out emotionally. He introduced me to a couple of people who were still there but preparing to leave. We went to his office. I sat in the chair. The office was small. Maybe 8x6'. A large window looked outside with a view of the parking garage.

When we got to his office, he sat down in his desk chair and proceeded to check his email. Once done, he asked me where we should go for dinner. So, he hadn't even thought of it. Which reminded me that this wasn't so much a "date night" as it was a chance for him to show off his work.

I hesitated in responding, he finally looked at me. I told him we needed to talk. He said, "About what?"

Ignoring, or perhaps just not wanting to see, any signals he should have heard in my voice. I told him, "I want a divorce." I remember saying it very quietly and he just stared at me. His body was still from shock, but I could see the emotions in his eyes as they slowly began to register the pain, the reality of what I said, and then the anger started to shoot out intensely.

He sat for a long time just staring at me. Angry. Speechless. Intimidating. Scary. Confused. He finally said something, I do not remember what, but he was angry. I remember the feelings. Fear, uncertainty, hating the angry, loud, mean, hurtful words. He stormed out of the office, I quickly followed him so I wouldn't get locked in.

At the parking garage, we separated to our own cars. He drove recklessly out, squealing tires and screeching through the place. I feared for his safety. Lord knows I had been in the car with him plenty of times when he drove this way and it felt out of control like we could crash at any moment.

I drove over to the Starbucks that was in the same office complex. That's as far as I could get before I completely broke down. I ended up calling each of the kids to tell them what happened. I started with Tony for two reasons: 1, as he was the oldest and 2, out of fear for his dad's safety. I remember telling him what I had told his dad. I will never forget Tony's calmness, compassion and sadness on the phone. Little did I know how I would crave that calmness and compassion over the next several months, even years.

I remember talking to Tony. He asked me why. I told him, "You don't know your dad like he used to be, you don't know us any way but arguing and fighting because things have been bad for that long." I told him we just couldn't make each other happy anymore.

I remember feeling helpless yet powerful. A strange combination to be sure. But I was helpless. Helpless to stop the wrenching pain I had inflicted on Brent, my sons and my daughters. But, powerful in the knowledge that what I was doing, the decision I had made and was now following through with, was the right decision for me. For my health, and ultimately for Brent's and for our family.

After talking further with Tony and finding out he could not get ahold of his dad, I tried reaching out to his friend Bob for help making sure Brent was safe. Bob was cold, as to be expected, but took my call and heard my concern. I can't remember for certain, but I think he tried to assure me Brent was fine and that it wasn't my worry anymore because I had made it thus. I ended up calling the police to get an APB on him for safety. I feared he would try to kill himself. He had made comments about doing so before, but always in the heat of an argument, not really anything I truly thought he would do.

Eventually, after hours of concern and worry, he showed up at the house telling us he had driven to the top of the parking garage and been sitting there the whole time.

Telling friends and family

I remember telling my sisters and a friend pretty quickly. I was counting on the friend to be my main support. Little did I know that just wouldn't happen because she always has her own issues, but I found two very good new friends. As well as bettering my relationships with my sisters, my divorce put me in a new place with my mom.

I had always been close to my mom. I remember telling her I would live with her forever, as many children do. But, as a sexually active teen, I pulled away from her. I was ashamed of my activities but didn't have the strength of the flesh to stop them. The spirit was willing, but my flesh was so very weak. Such a true statement for much of my life. Looking back, I can see that I was being groomed too. My boyfriend, to become my first husband, was slowly building a wedge between my mom and me. I wouldn't realize it until after the divorce.

Once in a counseling session while reflecting on my relationship with my mom, I stated that it was like her and Brent both wanted to control me. They would fight over who had control. That was inaccurate. My mom could see I was being controlled in a way that only a parent could see. She was trying to extract me from that. But I didn't know it was happening so I fought her attempts. After the divorce, I realized these things.

When I finally called my parents to tell them about the divorce, my mom said something I will never ever forget. She said, "I've been waiting 25 years to hear you say that."

That floored me. Stopped me in my tracks. Here I was, having spent so much time being anxious about letting them down by ending my marriage. Something that was not to be done, as marriage is for life. Period. No questions asked. But then she reacted this way. Really? Wow. I was speechless. No words. But, at the same time, I had an intense feeling of relief. I knew absolutely I had made the right choice for myself, my husband, my kids and the rest of my family. I knew it deep in my soul. Even if he didn't know it quite yet.

At the end of the marriage, at the time I made the decision, was a definitely feeling that a power shift had occurred. No more power struggle between the two of us. I had taken over and was no longer struggling with him. I was free and open to all the infinite possibilities of life now.

Granted I had children to care for, but three were adults and 1 was nearly. They were still my children. They needed my strength and quiet calmness. And I'd already gone through all my emotions. For me it was over, my feelings were all used up. It made me available to help my kids through this time as much as I could.

In July, we coexisted in the same house for 30 days while making arrangements for our new, separate lives. I was anticipating my new life of making my own decisions. Having complete control over everything, including things like how I dressed and what decor I used.

It was an intense, anxious time. I would not recommend it to anyone. We even slept in the same bed for the first week or 10 days, which was strange. I thought he would choose to sleep elsewhere, but he didn't. And neither did I. One day, after another fight over all of it, pointless and useless fights, I moved my things into my daughter's room. She was away most of that summer, so I used her space.

One morning he came barging in the room and grabbed my laptop and some other things, claiming they belonged to him. At first, I got very upset, but quickly realized that's what he wanted. So, I stopped. Said ok, if you want or need that, it's fine. I figured I would just buy myself a laptop.

Well, he did that because he was convinced I was using it to cheat on him. Ha! This man who accused me, in front of our children, of not wanting sex enough to satisfy him is now worried I'm cheating on him with someone else. He didn't realize his own folly.

Eventually he gave me back the laptop. And eventually we moved out separately from one another.

Labor Day

Over the weekend of Labor Day that year, during our separation, Peter spent the night at his friend's house on Friday night. I decided to go out and have some fun too. I contacted a new friend I had made and went to his place. We watched a movie, had a few beers and I stayed overnight.

As I was driving home the next morning, I had several anxious text messages and calls from the kids. They all were completely upset, losing it really. Their father was threatening to kill himself unless I sat down and talked with him. I had no desire to do this as my feelings were dead, my decision made, we were done. I wasn't looking back. All the attentions he had tried to pay to me during the last 2 months were just "too little, too late".

Reluctantly, I called Brent. I remember we argued severely on the phone and I eventually agreed to let him come to my house. I told him he needed to give me an hour. I knew I was 30 minutes out and wanted time to get in and settled before he arrived.

True to form, he did not respect that time frame and was waiting for me when I arrived. I pulled onto the driveway and grabbed two lawn chairs from the trunk. I made him sit on the driveway because I did not want his negative, narcissistic energy in my safe place.

We sat down facing each other and he just sits silently staring at me. I can tell he is highly emotional and it appears to me he is angry. But I sit, waiting for him to say something. This too is true to form as during our marriage, he would often grow silent and just refuse to discuss issues. But now I have the strength of my convictions that divorce is the right thing to do for us. And the behavior he exhibited, by drawing our children in to this, confirmed to me that I did make the right choice.

He finally starts to talk saying how much he misses me. I don't even remember reacting. I'm sure some people would have said my behavior during the meeting was cold and harsh. While I wouldn't necessarily disagree with them, I would say I had every right to be cold and harsh too. Of course, in these situations, we all think our personal stance is the right one.

So I decided to hear him out. I asked him what it was about me that he missed. He mentioned my cooking, the way I kept the house (which I'm sure I scoffed at) and that he missed having me in bed with him. I remember saying back to him, "You need a cook, a maid and a whore." Honestly! He didn't say anything uniquely me was what he missed. He could hire someone to meet those three needs. It wasn't me he missed, but what I did for him that he missed. After more circular conversation, he finally got in his car to leave. After sitting in my driveway for quite some time, he finally actually left. It wasn't until he had turned the corner at the end of the block that I got up and went inside.

I called the children, told them I had met with their dad and told them as much as they needed to know about how the conversation went. And went on about the rest of my day.

Work Incidents

Even moving out didn't stop him from trying to "get me back" The thing he really truly did not understand was that he had blown all the chances and opportunities. But I was emotionally checked out and had been for some time, so these things were just annoying and eventually scaring me.

He sent a bouquet of flowers. That little gift of appreciation you always hope you'll get, something special just on a random day. To know he loves you, wants to be with you, loves your life together. After I moved out, he finally sent that bouquet I'd been wanting for years. I had been asking, I mean straight out saying, why don't you send me flowers anymore? I would love to have flowers just because. Even if they were picked up from the grocery store on the way home. Just a special something.

Years I said this to him. And nothing until after I told him I wanted a divorce, moved out of our bedroom, ended the lease on our home, moved all my stuff to a new place, moved into that new place and had been there for nearly a month! Then he sends me a bouquet with chocolates and a little teddy bear. Now he's going overboard because he never thought I should be eating chocolates, would criticize me for doing so. To the point I had to hide what I ate and when. An unfortunate habit I'm still trying to lose.

The receptionist called me up to receive the flowers and was excited for me when I came up. But I quickly advised her I was not interested in receiving them and that she was welcome to do whatever she wanted with them. She looked at me like I'd grown a third eye. I'm serious, I told her. Really do not want them or the chocolates or the bunny, share them with the team. I asked her who delivered them and from her description it sounded like it was my ex.

I reached out to him, again, this time asking him to not come to my place of employment again. I had no desire to speak to him while at work and asked him to respect that as I would do the same for his employer.

Apparently he thought I was joking or at least that I wouldn't stick to my guns. A few days later, I went to the parking garage at the end of the day to find my car covered with more than 100 yellow sticky notes—inside and out. Each note said something about a dream or goal we'd had, good times we had shared, a hope we shared. On the steering wheel was the pièce de résistance. It said, "I Love You."

Thank goodness I had a co-worker walking out with me because it really scared me to have this happen. To know he could get into my car anytime, because he still had the key code for it, was very eye-opening and a bit frightening after this incident. At first, I was just stunned and didn't know what to do. At some point, it came to me to call the police. I don't know if my co-worker suggested it or if I thought of it, but it sounded like a good idea.

The Cobb County police came and took the report. They suggested getting a restraining order against him. I just didn't know for sure if I should or not. I knew I wanted him to stop but that sounded a bit drastic. Upon further conversation with the police, and a talk about how these were things Lifetime movies are made of, I agreed it was a good idea and started the process.

Cable Box Catastrophe

He called me at work on a random afternoon saying he needed his cable T.V. box back immediately. I found that interesting since I'd had it for a few months and he didn't seem to need it until that day. He didn't have any issue with leaving it in the house we shared and said he had all his stuff out. But, whatever, it's something I wasn't using so he could have it. But I sure didn't want to meet him alone at my house after the last time he came over.

I called Tony, my eldest child, to see if he could and would be willing to meet his dad to give him the cable box. Tony readily agreed so I made the arrangements with my ex and went about my day. My only stipulation was to meet him outside and not let him in the house. I simply didn't want his energy in that space. It was my place that I had made my very own and was very comfortable in it.

Around the meeting time, I got a frantic call from Tony. He was crying and could barely choke out, "Mom, I'm sorry. I didn't know he was going to do that." I finally settled him down enough to determine he was ok and didn't need immediate help from the authorities. I asked him to take a breath and start at the beginning with what had happened. I truly had no idea, no clue as to what was going on. And I never would have guessed what it he was about to say.

He begins to tell me how he got to the house and let himself in. His dad knocked on the door a short time later. Tony opened the door with the cable box in hand, intending for his dad to take the box and leave, as I had instructed. The next thing he knew, he was shoved aside as his dad hightailed it up the stairs.

Tony followed him telling him he needed to leave, asking what he was doing. Begging him to go, he didn't belong there. His dad picked up the laptop I used at the time and dug through my dresser until he found the gun he had given me for Christmas the year before. A gift I had not asked for—typical gift-giving for a narcissist. Give something that says more about him and less about the recipient.

He grabbed these two items and the cable box and went back out the door. That's when Tony called me. Poor kid felt so guilty for letting his dad in and was absolutely shocked at his dad's behavior to do such a thing. Barge into someone else's home and steal their possessions.

I was furious. So angry, more angry than I think I had been up to that point. For him to have done that to our son! The feelings of frustration and rage coursed through me while I searched for the right thing to say to Tony as this was clearly not his fault even though he felt he had let me down. I was finally able to tell Tony that I was not considering this his fault at all in any way, shape or form. This was beyond his control and he did all he could to make it better.

After talking to my support crew (aka counselor and trusted friends) about it, I ended up filing a police report because I didn't know what else to do. The police told me to try to negotiate for the items to be returned to me and advised they'd be happy to facilitate a meeting to make sure everything went smoothly at an exchange.

So, I started to reach out to him. Of course, at first he wouldn't even reply. Eventually I pestered him enough that he answered me. When he did finally answer, he agreed to return my things if I would meet him with no police. I don't recall even telling him about the police conversation so that was an interesting condition. I told him that I was not willing to forego having someone there to keep the peace and safety.

Obviously, we couldn't count on how he would behave since he had taken some of the actions he had. After 36 hours of negotiating, we agreed to meet the following day at the Outlet Shoppes of Atlanta. I immediately called the police about it and asked for an escort which they assured me they would provide.

The next day I woke as nervous as a wet bunny on a tightrope above an electric fence. I called on my support crew to get me through this as I had an untold number of times previously. The time to meet approached so I headed to the meeting spot to talk with the officer beforehand.

When I arrived at the Outlet Shoppes, there were very few people there as it was before opening time. I parked in the large lot behind McDonald's and the police car pulled up shortly after me. We spoke for a few minutes and I spotted Brent's car in the McDonald's parking lot. I could just feel him watching. Roaring in as fast as his car would go, he came to a screeching halt directly behind the police car and in front of mine.

He proceeded to whip the car door open and hold his hands up in the air with the gun in one and the computer in the other. The police officer immediately started telling him to stay in his car and sit still, calm down.

But, true to his nature, he would not listen. He shoved the items at the officer in such a way that he had no choice but to grab them. Spun around and got back in his car and spun his tires as he flew out of the parking lot. The officer had a few choice words for him but in the end we were both glad the exchange had taken place without serious incident.

I was so proud of myself for working through this process calmly and effectively. The results were exactly as I had hoped: I had my possessions back and no one was physically harmed.

Of course, there were concerns about Brent having my computer for 36 hours. I asked my favorite IT guy at work to wipe the computer and reload it for me. I didn't trust Brent at all when it came to the possibility of putting spyware or some kind of tracing software on the machine. It would be the type of thing he would do. Luckily, Chris was happy to help and took care of it quickly for me. He truly understood what I was dealing with since he was there when some of the incidents at work had taken place.

Once I was free of him daily and financially, I was able to save up a goodly sum and managed to come up with money for a lawyer, at a discount, but still. I wrote up the divorce paperwork myself and filed it. If it wasn't for the fact that Brent hired an attorney after the gun and computer incident, I never would have. But, once he did it, I felt I had to in order to see myself protected. In the end, it was actually reassuring to know that the lawyer had to keep my best interests, my safety, as his foremost concern.

I had visited Cherokee Women's Shelter a month or so before in order find out how to obtain the restraining order. I went back to them now and filed the request with the court. I also asked how to hire an attorney and if I could get some sort of discount since I had all the paperwork completed and filed.

They referred me to a lawyer in Canton who worked out an arrangement for me, and then, once he realized how much work I actually did, he lowered it even more. He contacted my ex's attorney and started working out details. My ex kept harassing me with obnoxious emails and texts. Making comments about how unfair the settlement was and he was right, it was unfair. I was taking the burden of the debts myself as well as not asking for any child support even though I would have our youngest child the majority of the time. But that's not how he saw it.

My attorney worked back and forth with his. I think the last straw was when we had everything worked out my ex added that he now wanted me to pay pet support and for pet bills since he now had both dogs. Not gonna happen.

My attorney pushed back hard and they finally finished the process. They wrapped up the negotiations and then, when I got his final bill, he had lowered it even more. I'm pretty sure that was his way of helping me after 23 years with this "tool", as he called Brent.

The paperwork was initially filed on October 17th (my birthday) and was finalized, signed by the judge on December 17th (my dad's birthday). A mere two months later. Mostly because we had no assets to fight over and I had agreed to take the bulk of the debt, there wasn't too much hassle.

Becoming Me

The divorce was the single most difficult decision I ever had to make in my life. I don't remember struggling that much when I found out I was pregnant with my first child. Of course, I was much younger, and much more naive.

This time, I knew the fallout of this decision could forever alter so many lives and my own, possibly in negative ways. As such, it was hard to make that final call, but I did because I became convinced it was the only way I could truly be me and that Brent could truly have a shot at being happy. I was not providing what he needed and knew now that I never would be able to.

I took this decision very seriously. I spent years in contemplation, prayer, journaling, researching, discovering and exploring. I had hoped to avoid divorce, but it seemed inevitable now.

Once I decided in my mind that it was the right decision, I slept on it for weeks to make sure I had no remorse about the choice. I kept seeing the future in bright possibilities as opposed to bleak and gray. The only anxiety I felt about the choice had to do with telling Brent, not with the choice itself.

I can only attribute this to truly becoming me and listening to myself. I do know that God was in this decision and I believe that as much as I know God hates divorce, He hates to see his children suffer even more.

In fact, the last couple years, I've wondered if marriage is really something that was intended by God or more so made up by man. There are so many beautiful things God put in place that have been perverted by man that it wouldn't surprise me to find out that was the case.

Setting boundaries for myself for what behavior was acceptable was empowering. Setting boundaries can show you how to respect yourself. If you go outside of those boundaries, the typical feeling is one of disappointment, even disgust. But staying within those boundaries, your own strength continues to rise to the point of feeling invincible.

Chapter 6

Dating

I've been on my own for a little while now and I think I'm ready to explore dating. This is a new experience for me. I was dating my ex at 15 (sorry Mom) and married at 19 and now, I'm 41. Never really dated around. I went out with a boy a time or two in high school, but that's it. Now is my time!

I started an account online and I'd gotten some interest. I'm not proud of everything that happened during this time, but it was a time of learning and exploration.

I really don't think it's necessary to get into my post-divorce dating adventures. Many were of the sort that using "adventure" to describe them would be complete overstatement. However, I do have some lessons learned and so I intend to describe only what is needed for those lessons to be relayed. No need to describe anything salacious, as if.

While exploring my new-found freedom after the end of my marriage, I discovered quite a bit about myself. One of those things is the metamorphosis I would go through each time I dated someone. I found myself changing the things I was most interested in and the thoughts and beliefs I expressed to more closely align with those of the man I was with. I realized, after doing so for about the fourth time, that I was not staying true to myself but was indeed changing as the wind. When I realized that about myself, I was so disappointed.

I dated one man for several months, but in the end, I broke it off because I felt we were just too different. I felt my kids would never respect him as my choice of mate and that would affect how I saw him. Truly, it was already affecting my view of him. So I broke up with him.

Months went by, during which time I dated occasionally here and there, but nothing too serious. I kept thinking of this first man. I couldn't seem to get past him. I thought about him all the time. I remember thinking at one point "Satan, get behind me, quit putting these thoughts in my head." No matter what I did, I couldn't seem to get past him though. I discussed my thoughts and feelings with my most trusted girlfriends and it seemed like the best choice was to call him up and see what he thought.

I reached out to him via text. And surprisingly he responded quickly. He said he had not been able to stop thinking of me either. We texted quite a bit that first night and eventually made a plan to meet. He picked me up and I can still remember that feeling of giddiness, that childlike joy, of seeing him again after all these months.

We started dating again and I told my kids I was seeing him. I told myself that no matter what my kids thought, this was my life and my choice. We started talking about the future. He had been shopping for a house to buy and now I joined him in that search. We moved very quickly, way too quickly.

I found myself compromising again. Acquiescing to whatever I thought he would be most amenable to. He did the same. Neither of us was really happy because we were both compromising so much. We were reacting to the situation with desperation really. We each were worried about being alone and therefore we did what we could to avoid having that happen. That is the worst reason in the world to be with someone.

Our relationship became so bad at one point that I had convinced myself moving 30 miles away from my children and working in a job that didn't utilize or appreciate my talents and skills was what was best. Boy howdy, was I wrong.

After just a couple months of this arrangement, I went to my doctor to recalibrate my anti-depression medication as I felt it was no longer effective. We worked on that for a few months, learning that Vyvanse is not a good option for me as it led quickly to my first ever panic attack. For all of you who suffer from anxiety or are prone to these attacks, my heart truly goes out to you. I cannot imagine living with that for long. How courageous you are.

After a time, my doctor and I found the right combination of medicine finally. But by then, the relationship I was in had crumbled to a point that I didn't even recognize it. I didn't know how to get out of it. I didn't have the courage or conviction to do so. I wasn't connected closely enough with my sweet Lord to have His strength either, at least I didn't think so anyway. The walls started caving in around me and I felt there was just no way to right the wrong turns I had taken on my current "adventure", if you will. I felt so despondent, so sad, that one night I cried, desperately, the entire way home after work.

When I got home, I went straight to bed, and cried most of the night. The man I was with was most concerned and tried to help. He encouraged me to go to the hospital as he feared I would find a way to harm myself.

I remember telling him I was glad I had sold my gun because I was afraid if I had it, I would use it on myself. Now I know I would never do that to myself, or to my children, grandchildren and family. But I can certainly see how that scared him so badly that night. Honestly, it scared me to feel that way and to feel it so intensely that I voiced my feelings.

My admission eventually led to my brief stay at a private psychiatric hospital. During that time, my biggest fear was missing my daughter's college graduation, but I did safely make it in time.

While staying at the hospital, I asked my sons to pack my things from the home I had been living in with the man who put me in the hospital so that I would not have to go back again. He did what he thought was best in the situation, but he was clearly not truly in love with me any more than I was with him. Upon my release, I went to my son's home and eventually found my footing and a better path for my life.

This may seem like an extreme and you may even think that there's no way you would get to that point. But I guarantee you, I never thought I would either! It was a series of small choices, one after another, that built on each other and locked me into a situation where I couldn't extract myself.

I learned a lot from this relationship. The most important thing I learned is that my kids and grandkids are more important to me than any other humans on the earth. I learned that God gives us infinite chances at doing life in a way that is pleasing to Him. I learned that love can be fickle, that compromising everything about myself is not actually love and that caring for another person to be happy is not a good enough reason to change your entire life.

At the time these events occurred, I had been a mom for 25 years. I had dedicated my time, talents and resources completely and wholly to my kids' growth and well-being. Why was I changing all that for this one person? I realized that the "right" person wouldn't require that of me. I am grateful every day that God stepped in and saved me from myself in this moment. I have always had so much life to live and love to give and joy to experience and sorrow to share with others, but I got lost inside my own misery, my own mind.

Please do NOT hold back these feelings. Get them out and keep talking about them until you find a way past them or someone to help with them. If you ever feel this way, please reach out to a suicide prevention hotline, a friend, a neighbor, your Uber driver, a co-worker, anyone at all.

A New Start

After staying with my eldest son and his wife for a few months, I had stabilized my emotions and saved enough money to work on finding a new home for myself. I had decided it needed to be affordable enough I could pay the rent with unemployment compensation and still afford my car. This is how I realized I needed to be able to completely and fully take care of myself. I had always had some sort of partner. Now it was truly on me and I was finally acknowledging this to myself.

In February of 2016, I moved into a 2-bedroom, 1.5-bath mobile home on Main Street in Kennesaw. That first night was the hardest night of my life. I had never lived alone before and here I am at 44, doing so for the first time ever. So many things in my life were not the way I planned them to be. But that's kind of how my life had always been. I've not been a big planner per se. I never felt settled enough to do so. I don't know if that was because of the marriage issues or was just me, my personality.

I found myself sitting alone in the living room of my new home. Cold and exhausted after a long day of moving in. There were soft spots and holes in the floor where the only thing keeping it from falling through was the carpet. I'd already found several dead bugs to clean up and the windowsills were coated with black dirt which I just prayed wasn't mold.

No microwave in the place and you could not open the oven door more than about halfway because it would hit the handle of the fridge. Probably wouldn't be baking or cooking much anyway because I didn't really know how to cook for just one. I've always cooked for at least 2 but then I was just starting out and we had little money. It was easy to cook small, simple meals. Through the years, I've had to cook for 6 and often extras. I do enjoy entertaining and cooking, but that won't be happening in this tiny place.

The moving in process was much easier on this move than so many others because over the past 3 ½ years, I had purged so very many belongings in all the moves. I just hoped I wouldn't wish some of those things back. My kids had made fun of me for so many things I kept through the years. Just wait until they have kids and want to see or even use some of those things. Then they'll be sorry for my purging. Let's be honest though, it's more the griping from the boys who wouldn't care about the sentimental things as much as the girls will anyway.

The first night was the hardest. I literally cried myself to sleep. I stayed up much later than I probably should have and the day had been emotional and exhausting. I certainly didn't do myself any favors. I was scared though. Truly the first time I had lived alone was a frightening process at this point in my life. I sobbed so hard that night. The feeling of being all alone in the world was pervasive. I knew intellectually I was not alone, but my feelings told me otherwise. This was the first time I consciously realized that my feelings would lie to me.

The next morning, when I woke up, I was determined to make a good start. Turning on the shower, I let the water warm up while I looked through my clothes. After a bit, I realized the water was hot, so I got in and started taking care of my business. Well, before I could even wet my hair, the water turned freezing. So shockingly cold! I adjusted the dials, trying desperately to get some heat. No luck at all. Not one drop of warmth was coming out of the faucet. I gave up, climbed out of the shower and, as I toweled off, the tears started to flow. Here I was, day one of my new life and I couldn't even take a shower! How was I possibly going to take care of myself?

I had no choice but to get to work that day. So, on my third day with no shower, dry shampoo caking my hair and wearing whatever I could find, I made it through that day. That night, I cried again as I went to bed, but it was not quite as long or as hard. Each day, I was able to survive a bit easier. And I figured out that this mobile home has a tiny water heater tank so no running water to get the hot stuff. Turn it on and jump in. Some lessons are quicker to learn than others.

As I moved into this new place physically, I found myself in a new place emotionally as well. I purposely chose this rental because I knew that even if I found myself unemployed, I could still pay the rent with the unemployment funds. I would also be able to save some money for emergencies due to this low rent. It really had the ability to put me in a good place financially and mentally. I could survive financially on my own here. I had the means to do so.

Next item to work on would be me. Teaching myself to know who I am at my very core as opposed to following the most recent emotion flitting through my atmosphere. Living alone allowed for more quiet time, reflection, prayer, thoughts than I had ever allowed or experienced before. Now I know that was the truly scary part for me. It wasn't so much being physically alone as it was being emotionally alone.

One man I dated told me that he had learned years ago that each of us must first be comfortable with our own self before we can try to share that comfort with others. At the time, I remember thinking that made sense. But now, in my quiet little home, I could truly find out if I was comfortable keeping my own silence. I was not.

I decided that I needed to take a good amount of time, at least 6 months, maybe a year or more, to just be me. I needed to learn what I was about, what I truly liked, believed and desired. I remember thinking I should experience all the seasons and holidays on my own before trying to venture into any kind of romantic relationship.

After 10 months of learning to love myself as I was and finding ways to move forward in my life, I felt truly ready to explore the possibility of finding a mate. Not dating, but actually finding a mate. I had been praying for some time and continued to do so. I really wanted God to find the right person for me. Not just any person who I thought might be a good choice, since my choices were not always the best, but God's are always full of infinite wisdom.

During this time, God spoke to me in dreams about my mate. He told me that he was preparing him for me just the same as I was being prepared for him. That created such excitement in me. The same excitement I believed I would feel upon meeting him.

Eventually I met the man who is today my husband. We met through an exclusive online service for professional adults. I actually reached out to him first, which I think has been important for me to be able to feel in control of myself during this process. My feelings of excitement have not wavered to this day. Whenever I think of that first meeting and how I felt watching him walk down the sidewalk toward me, I get goosebumps all over again.

God gave me another chance and I was in tune enough with Him to be able to know when to act and when to sit.

Nothing in this relationship was pushed or forced, I have been able to maintain myself and ideas. I've only had to compromise on things that are not of great importance. There is no call for me to compromise on my strong beliefs and ideals because my husband shares them. God truly prepared him for me and me for him.

Becoming Whole

Don't be fooled, I did not become whole because I found a man to share my life with. Quite the opposite. I became whole by listening to what I needed and what God had for me. I became whole by honoring myself, by learning about myself in a way I hadn't done for years.

Our current society uses the phrase "always be humble and kind" to share this same sentiment. By humbling ourselves to receive love and be comforted, we can then share that kindness with others. Being kind is a choice we can make to purposefully impact our little corner of the world.

Having a purpose for these times of discomfort, pain and sorrow helps to lessen the burden that could be brought upon us.

When we see that mom in the store whose child is seemingly out of control, instead of glaring at her, maybe a nice smile would be more kind.

The "so that" principle tells us that God will provide comfort in our time of need **so that** we can share that same comfort with others. As this book draws to a close, that is the one lingering thought I hope to leave with you.

Whatever you are currently going through, whatever you have gone through in the past, whatever you will walk through in the future, these situations are all meant to be used to draw comfort from God. Once we receive that comfort, the intention is for us to share that comfort with others.

Your "So That" Story

As you've read my experiences and "so that" moments, you may have had several *aha* moments concerning events in your own life. I would love to hear from you and encourage you.

Join the *So That* Facebook community, connect with others, and share your "so that" moments with other like-minded individuals.

Join here: www.facebook.com/sothatbook/

You can further connect with me by liking me on my Facebook page: www.facebook.com/sothatauthor/

Thank You

Thank you so much for reading my journey.

I would love to have your feedback which will help both myself and others who could benefit from the book.

Please take just a moment and leave a review on the Amazon book page.